The Greenmarket Cookbook

VIKING

75 years

The Greenmarket Cookbook

Joel Patraker and
Joan Schwartz

Recipes, Photographs by
Tips, and Lore Marry Kim
from the World
Famous Urban
Farmers' Market

Viking

VIKING
Published by the Penguin Group
Penguin Putnam Inc., 375 Hudson Street,
New York, New York 10014, U.S.A.
Penguin Books Ltd, 27 Wrights Lane,
London W8 5TZ, England
Penguin Books Australia Ltd, Ringwood,
Victoria, Australia
Penguin Books Canada Ltd, 10 Alcorn Avenue,
Toronto, Ontario, Canada M4V 3B2
Penguin Books (N.Z.) Ltd, 182-190 Wairau Road,
Auckland 10, New Zealand

Penguin Books Ltd, Registered Offices:
Harmondsworth, Middlesex, England

First published in 2000 by Viking Penguin,
a member of Penguin Putnam Inc.

10 9 8 7 6 5 4 3 2 1

LIBRARY OF CONGRESS CATALOGING-IN-PUBLICATION DATA

Patraker, Joel.
   The Greenmarket cookbook / Joel Patraker and Joan Schwartz;
   photographs by Marry Kim.
      p. cm.
   ISBN 0-670-88134-1
   I. Cookery. 2. Farm produce—New York (State)—New York. 3.
Farmers' markets—New York (State)—New York. I. Schwartz,
Joan, 1938– II. Title.

TX715 .P3169 2000
641.5—dc21   99-053639
This book is printed on acid-free paper. 8

Printed in the China
Set in Times New Roman and Truth
Designed by Jaye Zimet

Joel Patraker To Marry Kim, my loving wife, partner, soul mate, muse, fellow dreamer, and modern-day Gracie Allen: If not for your constant encouragement, help, and support, our book would have stayed a dream and would never have become a reality. As for your beautiful photographs—without them I would have very few stories to tell. Marry, when you smile at me, the world is a beautiful place. "Hey, Marry! Tell me again, ya. Where did I find you?" ❦ To Fran Patraker, my sister: Franny, you are always there for me. Every time I stumble and another step seems impossible, you convince me that it's not. For that, as well as a thousand other kindnesses, I love you. Samuel, Franny's son and our first nephew—I'll race you to the top of the Statue of Liberty any time you want. ❦ To Rose and Joseph Rolfe, my wonderful grandparents: Grandpa, you taught me to love playing and planting in the soil and to respect and appreciate the harvest of my labors; and that rhubarb wouldn't kill me and wild apples can be delicious. Grandma, you cooked with only the freshest ingredients— Grandpa wouldn't have had it any other way. If it came in a can or a box, it probably didn't belong in your kitchen, and, as my patient wife will confirm, it has no place in mine, either. Your inspiration serves as a constant reminder to me that helping other people is a responsibility, not a chore; and that there is always room at the table for the unexpected guest. Not a day goes by without my feeling your warmth from above as I sweep the sawdust off the market floor.

Marry Kim To the loving memory of my mother, Doo Sook Kim.

Foreword

In October 1988, I joined the staff of the Union Square Cafe as executive chef. To help me get acquainted with my new home, Danny Meyer, the restaurant's young and very enthusiastic owner, was especially fond of taking me for a stroll now and again through the Union Square Greenmarket, just a half block away from our door. ❦ Danny explained that the location of his then three-year-old restaurant had been largely decided by its proximity to the market. The open-air farm stands piled high with fresh, seasonal produce reminded him of the wonderful outdoor markets he had known while living in Rome some years earlier.

In my six years of cooking in France, Switzerland, and Italy, I too had experienced the pleasure of dealing directly with farmers and their just-picked produce. It was very exciting to know that the Union Square Cafe had its own enchanted garden, just a short walk away.

Well before I joined the restaurant, a relationship had developed between the Union Square Cafe kitchen and the farmers. My sous-chefs introduced me to the different stands and familiarized me with their wares. It was at this point that I first met Joel Patraker.

Joel was then Greenmarket's special projects coordinator, but the title didn't really mean much to me. What did impress me was his passion for and dedication to Green-

market. Joel had boundless enthusiasm for spreading the gospel of support for local agriculture. I came to rely on his expertise, whether it was to source out a particular fruit or vegetable or to make the acquaintance of a farmer. In the ensuing years, our relationship has deepened.

In *The Greenmarket Cookbook,* Joel shares his passion with all of us. The book is a charming blend of delightful anecdotes, useful facts, delicious recipes, and Greenmarket lore. It is, in the true spirit of the market, a collection of the work of many hands, lovingly assembled by Joel, curator of Greenmarket treasures.

—MICHAEL ROMANO
Executive Chef, Union Square Cafe
New York City

Preface
An Homage to Mahlon Budd

At six o'clock on an unseasonably cold morning in 1983, I arrived at the Union Square Greenmarket to sell grapes—grapes grown by a man I did not know, on a farm I had never seen. I showed up early, hoping to make a good impression, but as I walked down the market aisles, all around me were stands that had probably been set up before sunrise. When I introduced myself to my new employer, Mahlon Budd, he was quick to tell me that there was no "Mister Budd" around here, but that if I was looking for a fellow named Mahlon who grew grapes in Dundee, New York, I had come to the right place. He had already unloaded the better part of a flatbed truck full of grapes.

Before I could finish apologizing for being too late to help unload the cases of grapes, Mahlon pushed back his straw hat (which, like his cigarettes, he was seldom without) and announced: "These are called lugs, and each lug holds about thirty pounds of grapes if you don't pack them too tightly, and you don't want to do that, because it damages the fruit.

"Lugs," he repeated, "you got that? Besides, you're not late for work. I didn't think a city boy would come to work any earlier than seven in the morning."

"Lugs," I answered, suspecting that this was just the first of many things that I would learn from Mahlon Budd. At that point, I was familiar only with grapes bought from the supermarket and the large green grapes that grew behind my family's house on Long Island. (He told me that the latter were Niagaras, a white variety of the Concords popular with home gardeners in the early 1900s.) In the months to come, he would patiently explain the differences among Diamond, Aurora, Concord, Caco, Catawba, and Worden grapes; the significance of *labrusca* and *vinifera;* which grapes were seeded and which were seedless; and the importance of the terms *foxy* (musky), *tart, sweet,* and *deeply perfumed.* I soon learned that nothing beats beginning a fall day with freshly pressed juice from Diamond grapes.

Every market morning, Mahlon would open the doors of his truck and let his radio loudly proclaim his love for jazz. Sometimes he got other farmers to tune their radios to the same station for a mini-concert that echoed down the market aisles. When he wasn't unloading or conducting, he was brewing coffee on his camp stove and passing out cups to other farmers and early-morning customers.

Mahlon was a little under six feet tall, with not an ounce of fat, and an easy smile. He drove more than four hours each way between his small vineyard in the Finger Lakes region of upper New York State and Union Square. Like his market neighbors, he had a passion for working the land and selling the fruits of his labors to "appreciative city people," as he called them.

As a merchant seaman, he had seen most of the world before settling down; and he had spent considerable time in the jazz clubs of downtown New York City. Many evenings after work, as we walked through the streets of Greenwich Village, he would point out storefronts that had once housed popular nightspots. On occasion, we would stop and have a beer at a bar that had seen better days, its past grandeur hidden under years of accumulated dust and spilled liquor. Mahlon would describe from memory where the piano had been or how sweet it was to hear Joe Williams sing.

Mahlon Budd fascinated me with his tales, and his memories guided me through the forgotten streets of the city I was born in. But the things that especially drew me close to Mahlon were his love of farming and his fondness for his fellow human beings.

I was intrigued by the way he and most of the other farmers interacted with their customers. Mahlon let me know that the true weight of a pound of grapes at his stand was always a pound and a quarter, if not more. No one was to leave the stand hungry, and if you were down on your luck, Mahlon always had time to hear your story and offer some assistance. Being with him was like stepping back in time to my grandfather's produce store in Richmond Hill, Queens, in a better, more caring era.

Regular customers would reciprocate Mahlon's interest each market day. "How's the harvest coming along?" "How was your drive to the city?" "Did you have much rain?" they would ask. It really mattered to them how the season was progressing; it touched something inside them, and something inside me, as well. Greenmarket was a place of coming together, a place to be with neighbors and strangers in a way that a big city does not normally allow.

After that season, I stayed on at Greenmarket and worked another harvest with my new friends. I eventually became its special projects coordinator and I am now assistant director. Mahlon Budd has since gone on to that "great vineyard in the sky," but before leaving, he captivated me and thousands of New Yorkers with his warm smile, delicious grapes, straw hat, good coffee, wild stories, and patient ways.

—JOEL PATRAKER
New York City

Acknowledgments

I am indebted to friends, farmers, customers, chefs, journalists, co-workers, and market enthusiasts from around the world. For making this book a reality, deepest thanks to: Jane Dystel, my remarkable agent, and her crew at Jane Dystel Literary Management. Joan Schwartz, my most steadfast collaborator. Sarah Baker and Dawn Drzal, my talented and supportive editors. Tracey Seaman, recipe tester extraordinaire. Katherine Alford, Sallie Han, Suzanne Hamlin, Tamara Holt, Nancy

Harmon Jenkins, Julia Jordan, Connie McCabe, Adam Rapoport, and Arthur Schwartz, my guiding lights.

Bill Telepan, Gray Kunz, Michael Romano, Maury Rubin, and Ilene Rosen, my culinary sounding boards.

For unlimited love, thanks to my family and friends:

The Hawaii Clan, "Oma" Kim, "Braddahs" Roy Miyamoto, Ron Oster, and Michael Pang and Aunties Donna and Linda Grimes.

Larry Gershberg, Glenn Teller, Alan and June Ginsberg, Lee and Angela, Arlene, Richard, Lisa, Michael Morrison, Dana Schwartz, and Jay Ellen Kerig.

The person whom I hold solely responsible for opening the door to my life at Greenmarket is my old friend Tony Mannetta, Greenmarket director, who introduced me to Mahlon Budd. Without Tony's constant friendship and enduring faith in me, my days at market would have ended long ago. Christine Mannetta, like my wife, Marry, continues to understand that she didn't just marry a man; she married the whole Greenmarket, for better or worse.

Thank you to Ronnybrook Farm Dairy for providing all the wonderful dairy products we used in testing these recipes and to Bernadette and Walter Bulich-Kowalski of the River Garden Farm for their super-helpful flower advice.

My gratitude to the Greenmarket staff, who continues to make it all happen: Peter Costello, Joe Cuniglio, Nell Downey, Laurel Halter, Carolyn Laser, Lynn Peemoeller, Tommy Strumolo, and especially Brendan Corr.

And special thanks to the Greenmarket farmers —without you, there is no story.

Contents

The Greenmarket Cookbook

The Union Square Greenmarket

A Little History

Barry Benepe, founder and recently retired director of Greenmarket, was an urban planner in the Hudson Valley in the 1970s when he first learned of the distressing situation of farmers there. Towns were mapping out their development and increasing their growth throughout the region, but no corresponding plans were being made for farmland. The small, family-owned farms that gave character and substance to upstate New York and that provided a livelihood for scores of hardworking farmers, and the fresh food the farms provided, were being threatened with extinction.

Barry's family, although they were not farmers by profession, had owned a working farm, and he remembered waiting in long lines at wholesale auction blocks, where farmers received low prices for their crops. His recollections of the perilousness of subsistence farming—along with the fact that, in his West Greenwich Village neighborhood, he could not purchase a ripe, locally grown peach during the heart of the season—helped him form a plan that would become the salvation of local agriculture. Farmers in the New York–New Jersey area would be able to sell their fresh, seasonal produce directly to customers through a network of markets located throughout New York City. The Greenmarket concept was born, and today's flourishing network of urban farmers' markets owes its existence to the vision of Barry Benepe and Bob Lewis, his professional associate.

The first New York City Greenmarket opened in the summer of 1976 on East Fifty-ninth Street and Second Avenue, and shortly afterward, it was followed by what has become the most famous and successful of the markets, the Union Square Greenmarket. Another market, in downtown Brooklyn, soon opened its gates, and today there are twenty-eight thriving Greenmarket locations in Manhattan, Brooklyn, the Bronx, Queens, and Staten Island.

Since its inception, Greenmarket has been a program of the Council on the Environment of New York City. Without the guidance and wisdom of the Council's honorary chairman, Marian S. Heiskell, and executive director, Lys McLaughlin, the 16,000 acres of regional farmland either cultivated or protected by Greenmarket participants would have long ago become office parks, or worse; and Greenmarket as we know it (as well as many other wonderful programs of the CENYC) would not exist.

The Union Square area, once depressed, experienced an exciting rebirth as a result of the market's success, with fine restaurants springing up near their source of fresh food and thousands of customers bringing a surge of new life to the neighborhood.

During the past seventeen years, I have worn out many a pair of boots walking the aisles of New York City's Greenmarkets and the fields and orchards of farmers. The Union Square location has grown from a small, quaint gathering of a few farmers and shoppers into a world-class outdoor farmers' market in the heart of the city. Today, Greenmarket farmers raise more than 75 varieties of apples, over 300 types of hot and sweet peppers, 40 kinds of lettuce, and 120 types of tomatoes (some of which are rare heirloom varieties)—among other produce. I have had the opportunity not only to watch the market grow but to see the children of the first generation of Greenmarket farmers come of age and take their places beside their parents at the stands and on the farms. I have shared meals with farmers and customers alike and

have learned the importance of seasonal foods and loving preparation. I have seen professional chefs stop phoning in their orders to wholesalers and start to explore the bounty of fresh produce.

One of many chefs in the market neighborhood, Maury Rubin of The City Bakery, sums it up well: "The market determined where I would locate my business, and my business uses the resources that the market provides. . . . Greenmarket has come to represent community in the best way. I am connected to something that a great many people understand and love."

The Greenmarket Tour

The moment you step inside its borders, any good farmers' market grabs you and envelops you in a

whirlwind of colors and aromas—the bright reds and yellows of ripe tomatoes, the purples, greens, and crimsons of grapes, the spicy bouquet of hot and sweet peppers. All around are tables covered with crisp greens, ripe melons, flowers and plants in every color of the rainbow, wildflower honey, maple syrup, cheese, ice cream, eggs, meats, poultry, bread, cider doughnuts, pot pies, wine—what's your pleasure? Here is a glorious Mardi Gras that will engage your senses and lift your spirits.

Our Union Square Greenmarket is a large urban enclave whose boundaries are set by the busy, noisy streets surrounding it. In contrast, your local market may be on a country road or in a quiet corner of any town or city. You may get there on foot or by car, rather than by subway or bus. But it will offer you the same sense of exhilaration that Greenmarket offers me, as you connect—perhaps more directly than you ever have before—with the earth, the people who till it, and its bounty.

A walk up and down the market aisles always jump-starts my day. Let me take you along, pointing out some of the farmers and their stands, highlighting the specialties, and sharing some tidbits of information I have gleaned in my years here.

Entering on a summer day, we are met by the cornucopia that is Alex and Linda Paffenroth's stand. Here are at least five or six varieties of radishes in red, pink, and pastel stripes; red, orange, and golden beets; red dandelions; many-colored eggplants; and bunching onions. If we were to visit in the early fall, there would be a dozen kinds of squash, as well. This is a great introduction to Greenmarket's way with vegetables, and many other stands echo the Paffenroths' bounty.

Depending on the season, ramps, fiddleheads, strawberries, and a dizzying variety of heirloom potatoes will tempt you at Rick and Nickie Bishop's Mountain Sweet Berry Farm (see Rick's story in Chapter 4). At S and SO Produce, owned by Stosh and Trudy Osczepinski, carrots, leeks, and celery are piled chest high (that's my chest, and I'm six-foot three). The towering displays are visible not only from the north entrance to the park but from the city streets beyond. Look for Cherry Lane Farms, where the Dare family brings us tender asparagus, early spring spinach, paper-skinned new potatoes great for roasting, and summer okra (see the Dares' story in Chapter 5). Migliorelli Farm, a premier grower of traditional and Italian greens, as well as melons, is another colorful stand with dazzling displays of produce (read about the Migliorellis in Chapter 2).

For more veggies, scout Doug and Sue McWhorter's Northern Borne Farms and their hydroponic (grown in water) bell peppers and seedless cucumbers. Don't miss Sycamore Farms, run by the Smith family, where the corn draws customers, six deep at times, eager to look, select, and ask questions. You'll be impressed by the Kirby pickling cucumbers, black and lavender eggplants, brightly colored bell peppers, and ripe field tomatoes (see the Smiths' story in Chapter 2). To complete your veggie immersion, be sure to stop by the Windy Maples Farm stand of Don and Ethel Keller (part of Greenmarket since 1976); and check out the delicate squash blossoms and baby lettuce at D'Attolico's Organic Farm stand.

If you are a fan of those crunchy little nutrient factories called sprouts, don't miss Hudson Valley Organic Gardens, where John Adams sells several varieties in the winter (he adds organically grown tomatoes, zucchini, and greens in the summer).

Leave some room in your basket for the mushrooms you will gather—oyster, shiitake, and cremini, among others—at the Bulich Mushroom Company. They are fresh and clean enough to make you forget Mom's advice to cut off the bottom of the stems.

Now work your way over to a stand that is among the most colorful In the market. Ted and Susan Blew, of Oak Grove Plantation, will show you a mind-boggling array of sweet and hot peppers, as well as heirloom tomatoes, grain, and meats (read more about the Blews and their crop in Chapter 2).

Scratch a Greenmarket customer and you'll find a tomato expert! This is where heirlooms are discovered and favorite varieties sought out—where you come to make a killing in Cherokee Purples, Banana Legs, and Green Zebras.

Tim and Jill Stark's Eckerton Hill Farm comes to market with the famous heirloom tomatoes that have graced the cover of *Gourmet* magazine, as well as colorful hot and sweet peppers (see the Starks' story in Chapter 2).

You can't miss the bright reds and golds at Fox Hill Farms, where "Wild Bill" Leritz displays tomatoes grown from seed he saves each year. Early on, Bill decided that he wanted his customers to think about his tomatoes, not just walk up to his stand and say, "I'll have some Brandywines." To that end, he refused to disclose any tomato names and referred to each type only by a number (you could buy number 15, number 32, and so on—but you had to look at it closely, first). Molly O'Neill wrote in *The New York Times* about how she grew some heirloom tomatoes from seed and jokingly named one of her varieties "Old Crank," after Bill himself.

If you inhale deeply, then follow your nose, the celebration continues as you find yourself facing Anne Salomon's Twee Fontein Herb Gardens. Among the flowering herbs on display is one of my favorites, English lavender, and I buy as many bags of it as I can. I like to keep some in my pockets and sprinkle it on friends' hands; or I put a generous bunch on my table just to keep myself in a good mood.

Then stroll over to the Stokes Farm stand where the Binaghi family sells fantastic herbs, as well as vegetables. Stokes is the informal meeting place for chefs, farmers, and staff who gather to discuss life, market, and family—fueled by Chef Bill Telepan's large boxes of doughnuts.

For an earthy counterpoint to the delicate aromas of lavender, sage, and thyme, visit Keith's Farm, where garlic is king. Keith Stewart grows some of the best I've ever tasted, and he has taught people that they can

eat not just the cloves but the garlic top too. He also sells a variety of herbs and lettuces and a lot of splendid greens.

Having planned your salad and veggie courses, it's time to supply yourself with juicy, ripe fruit for dessert and snacks. Along with the apples and apricots on your list, be sure to bring home some of the more unusual gems, such as white peaches and Seckel pears.

The Nicholson family's Red Jacket Orchards is a good place to start. Here, among the regular customers, we might find the editor in chief of *Gourmet* magazine, Ruth Reichl, selecting ripe apricots for a pie (see her recipe in Chapter 2). Ed and Carol Kesler of

Joel Patraker at the Atlantic and Flatbush Avenue Greenmarket, circa 1985

Peter Monroe

Tree-Licious Orchards bring their delicious and unusual peaches, heirloom apples, and apricots to market (see the recipe for Peach Coffee Cake on page 64), and the Lee family's Pittstown Fruit Farm introduces us to the Asian pear, shaped somewhat like an apple, with light yellow or golden brown skin. At last count, the Lees were growing a dozen varieties (along with peaches, apples, tomatoes, and bitter melons).

You have several more choices to help you fill your fruit bowl to overflowing: luscious fruit from Peter Hotaling's Clover Reach Orchards; Nemeth Orchard's plums and other fruits (as well as delectable applesauce); ripe fruit from Dick McGivney's Berry Knoll Farm stand (he sells potted begonias too); and Terhune Orchards' marvelous peaches and French Mirabelle plums.

Let's finish our orchard tour at the wise guy stand, the Kent family's Locust Grove Farms. Chip Kent is in charge, selling his "Locally Groan Fruit"—apples, quinces, pears, and cherries—and labeling them with his famous descriptions, such as "Drippy,

Spicy, and Aromatic" (read about Chip in Chapter 3). If you're lucky, you might get to buy one of the incredible apple pies baked by Helen Kent, Chip's mother—if not, make your own from Helen's recipe on page 123). Over fifty varieties of apples are sold here and there are always good samples and good vibes.

When is a grouch not a grouch? Most of the time, if he's "the Grouchy Gourmet," Jim Grillo of Northshire Farms (the story in Chapter 4 explains how he got the name). In the heart of the summer, Jim sells cultivated and wild blueberries, wild mushrooms, succulent watermelons, and muskmelons; and in the colder months, his stand looks very much like a French *marché* butcher shop.

Grapes are what first brought me to Greenmarket, and they may very well lure you, as well. In the upstate Finger Lakes region, Ken and Eileen Farnan of Buzzard Crest Vineyards grow the most interesting varieties of seeded and seedless organic grapes that you can buy in New York City. And Stone Arch Vineyards, where Kenny Barber presides, has been offering excellent grapes and grape juice for as long as I can remember.

Joel Patraker with Greenmarkets' future customers

You will find award-winning wines at two stands: Art Hunt's Hunt Country Vineyards and John Martini's Anthony Road Vineyards. Their wines are served at the Gramercy Tavern and Union Square Cafe, as well as at other fine restaurants. Stop by for a sample, if you're old enough.

In addition to satisfying us with food and drink, the market nourishes the eyes—and soul—with dazzling flowers and plants.

Chef Maury Rubin of The City Bakery with the author

The ground seems carpeted with row upon row of multicolored herbs and bedding plants in trays and pots; tables and shelves are bursting with even more varieties; and the vibrant buckets of flowers at James Durr's Sykesville Flower Farm can be seen from blocks away. Look for Duva Farms' tuberoses, the quintessential Hawaiian blooms, with their intoxicating fragrance of honey and butter; Michael Barry's Seven Pines Farm's heirloom roses, whose vivid colors and scents will amaze you; and the Faoro family's exotic potted amaryllis and lilies.

Adding to the panorama are the Cheerful Cherry Farm stand's scented geraniums, as well as cherries, mulberries, grapes, and late-season peaches; and the plants and flowers at Carvalho Greenhouses and Hodgson Farms (which also offers tomatoes and raspberries). Dick Hodgson remembers his first day at the East Fifty-ninth Street market, when his tables were knocked over by eager customers surging through the gates. Back then, the Hodgsons were selling eggs and corn, but they have since turned all their chicken coops, with running water troughs, into greenhouses.

Sparkling, golden honey has always drawn people to farmers' markets, and every part of the country offers its own specialties. Since honey varies in flavor, color, and perfume according to its flower source, you can find orange blossom honey in Florida and blueberry honey in Maine; and in Hawaii, coffee honey is a particular treat. In our neck of the woods, Walter and Noni Bauer's Twin Spruce Apiaries offer linden, buckwheat, wildflower, and clover honey, along with a variety of honey-sweetened treats (see Noni's recipe for Honey-Carmel Apples, page 118). And at David and Mary Graves's Berkshire Berries stand, you can buy true New York City honey, because David is that rare creature, an urban beekeeper. For a short time, he kept a hive of bees on the Greenmarket office roof; it has since been moved, but David still maintains some secret bee locations in the city. Berkshire also has maple syrup products and homemade jams.

Buck Hill Farms produces and sells maple syrup and other delicious maple products of high quality (see the Bucks's story in Chapter 4), and the Van Glad brothers, Tony and Andy, sell excellent maple products at their Wood Homestead Stand. Howard and Stephan Cantor of Deep Mountain Maple will introduce you to maple candy with hot peppers, ground ginger, and other exotic flavorings that range from "warm" to "knock your socks off" (see their Maple Syrup Tips, page 132).

If you are delighted when people prepare food for you, join me at Beth's Farm Kitchen, where Beth Linskey offers tempting jams, pickled items, and chutneys, among other treats. Her seedless black raspberry jam is irresistible!

Keep your eyes wide open and you'll discover that the market is much more than green. It's also a great place to stock up on dairy products, bread, eggs, poultry, meat, seafood, and, of all things, cloud-soft, vividly colored yarn.

Little Rainbow Chèvre offers tempting goat cheese such as Berkshire Blue and feta, goat yogurt, and, of course, goat milk. Try their samples! At the Ronnybrook Farm Dairy, someone from the family is always keeping tradition alive, providing milk in glass bottles, offering fall and winter customers fortifying hot chocolate, and tempting warm-weather shoppers with ice cream to die for. Ronnybrook produces dairy products with no growth hormones.

Wild Bill Leritz of Fox Hill Farm and Ken Barber of Stone Arch Farms

Coach Dairy Goat Farm, owned by Miles and Lillian Cahn and their daughter, Susi (who is married to Chef Mario Batali), displays goat cheese, yogurt, and yo-goat yogurt drink, among other products. Coach Farm goat cheese is ladled by hand into tapered molds, as opposed to the extrusion method, and you can notice the difference in texture and taste. And Hawthorne Valley Farm sells biodynamic cheese, yogurt, bread, meat, and quark, a subtly flavored cream cheese–like spread seldom seen outside of farmers' markets (see page 59 for Onion Lovers' Dip).

At this point, if you start to long for a hunk of crusty fresh bread to eat with some of that cheese, Rockhill Bakehouse offers quite a few temptations, and Don Lewis's Wild Hive Farm Bakery sells very good honey-sweetened baked goods—his corn bread is excellent.

When you shop at a farmers' market, forget everything you've ever learned about eggs. There are many more options than just white or brown; small, medium, or large; and chicken; and you won't find better or fresher quality unless you raid the coops yourself at dawn.

Be sure to visit Morse Pitts's Windfall Farms stand for blue-shelled Araucana chicken eggs, whose flavor and quality are as remarkable as their color (and for exotic lettuces and micro greens, as well). Fred Price and Faye Chan of The Fifth Floor Kitchen sell the eggs of free-range game birds and use many of these unusual eggs in their baked goods. At the Knoll Krest Farm stand, Bob and Alice Messerich sell both the chicken and the egg—brown and white free-range eggs and excellent free-range chickens, whole or in parts.

Look for fresh duck, goose, pheasant, and wild turkey eggs at Quattro's Poultry and Game Farm stand,

Pat Osip of Stan-Pat Farms

where the Quattrociocchi family also sells free-range pheasants, wild turkeys, capons, and guinea hens, as well as pheasant sausage and scrumptious turkey and chicken pot pies. (See Joyce's recipe for Roasted Wild Turkey with Bread Stuffing, page 108). Peaches from their beautiful peach orchard are an unexpected treat.

The Union Square Greenmarket may look land-locked, but don't be fooled—few places offer such easy access to the high seas. Alex Villani's Blue Moon fish and seafood stand brings a variety of sparkling fresh fish to the market, and the lines of customers are long and enthusiastic. Alex is joined by his wife, Stephanie (see her intriguing take on Greenmarket in Chapter 3). Visit Jack Gunn (aka Captain Jack Flash), with partner Richie Puza, at the Point Lookout Fish Company. Jack is an experienced and knowledgeable fisherman, and the quality of his seafood is unbeatable (read about Jack's adventures in Chapter 4). At Eden Brook Aquaculture, Rissa and Jon Wallach sell the gleaming fresh trout that they raise in Catskill Moun-tain–fed streams. You haven't had trout until you've tried theirs! And at Atlantic Lobster Company, Paul Schultz brings us high-quality lobster and other deli-cious seafood. The Doxsee Sea Clam stand is the source of savory baked clams, clam puffs, and frozen chopped clams, and Bob Doxsee is the source of much Greenmarket lore (see Chapter 4).

Two stands sure to capture your interest sell both lamb and beautiful yarns: Barbara Hillsgrove's Wooly Hill Farm; and Whippoorwill Farms, owned by Mal-colm and Linda Maclaren. Linda acts as knitting in-structor every day she's at market, and she also will knit things to order.

When you've finished that satisfying market-fresh meal, what can you do with the inevitable table scraps, kitchen and garden cuttings, and other biodegradables at your house? Greenmarket has the answer! Bring them down to the Lower East Side Ecology Center's stand and Christina Datz and Clyde Romero will have them composted (but no animal products, please). And as a contributor, you can get back compost for your own potting soil or garden. Trust Greenmarket to guide you through the cycles of nature, from start to finish.

At this point, tour completed, you should be feel-ing a little tired, and considerably elated. Now it's time to open *The Greenmarket Cookbook.*

How to Use This Book

How exciting it was for me to learn that the word *season* has its origins in the Latin word for sowing: since ancient times, farmers have planted seeds in har-mony with the cycles of nature and have harvested crops and eaten fruits, vegetables, and grains accord-ing to the same cycles. Today, the resurgence of greenmarkets and farmers' markets is giving us the opportunity to return to the seasons and the earth.

Not surprisingly, this book is organized according to season. Each chapter introduces a season at the market, then presents a shopping list of what farmers will offer during that period.

The items in these lists are not arranged alphabetically, as you might expect. Instead, under each category (Salad and Cooking Greens, Vegetables, and so on) they appear in order of their harvest, so that gooseberries precede garlic tops, and summer squash precedes corn. Nor are the seasons strictly what your calendar would lead you to expect. Summer at the market means July, August, and September; fall is October, November, and December; winter is January, February, and March; spring is April, May, and June. These are the farmers' seasons here in the Northeast.

Each list is a simple introduction that will get you fired up and ready to shop for old favorites and new discoveries—but what exactly is "anise hyssop?" For fuller information on each entry, see the Appendix, where market edibles are listed alphabetically and described.

Useful charts for interesting categories of vegetables or fruits are also part of each chapter, as are fruit and vegetable tips and anecdotes about the people you will meet at market. Finally, you will find recipes that are easy to follow and written for people like me who are not professional chefs, but who enjoy making fresh, exciting meals at home for family and friends. All this aims to give an understanding of what it means to cook and eat meals based on local growing seasons.

The section *For All Seasons* that ends this chapter offers "Filling Your Market Basket Year-Round," a

Shoppers

list of Greenmarket stalwarts that are always available. It also contains "The Greenmarket Pantry," with recipes for Vegetable Bouillon, Chicken Stock, and piecrust; and directions for roasting peppers—all useful for preparing the dishes in the chapters that follow.

On your next trip to market, use this book as your guide. Review the recipe list for each chapter or scan the index to find a recipe or key ingredient that excites your imagination and your palate. Write out your shopping list and take it along. But leave yourself time and space for spontaneity. Prepare to give in to the temptations you surely will find.

You may arrive with five things on your list, when suddenly, your attention is caught by some golden beets, sparkling in the sun. You're being reeled in, and you're hooked when the farmer offers you a sliver to taste and it is moist on your lips, sweet on your tongue. Now there will be six things in your shopping basket, not five. You pass a few more stalls and another farmer casts her line in your direction. "How are you doing today?" she calls out. "I see you've got a lovely bunch of beets. How are you going to cook them?" You respond, "I haven't decided yet." The farmer continues: "I have some fresh rosemary here today. My mother always cooked her beets by roasting them with a little rosemary. Delicious!" Caught again! You pass the farmer a dollar bill for another spontaneous purchase, and walk down the aisles, rubbing a sprig of herb between your fingers and raising it to your nose for a glorious whiff.

Good farmers' markets overcome shopping lists—and traditional approaches to cookbooks. Consequently, I encourage you to use this book as raw material, the paint or clay that will be the basis for your culinary masterpiece. Whatever the season, browse through the market basket list, charts, and recipes; they will help you understand what seasonal cooking is all about. Then, with recipes in mind and senses alert, let the market help you decide what's for dinner or lunch.

Filling Your Market Basket Year-Round

Sprouts	*Salad Greens*	*Dairy*	*Poultry, Meat, and Game*
Radish	Microgreens	Whole Milk (Cow, Goat)	Chicken
Broccoli		Skim Milk	Beef
Onion	*Eggs*	Buttermilk	Pork
Sunflower	Chicken	Heavy Cream	Scrapple
Daikon		Half-and-Half	Sausage (Pork, Rabbit,
Buckwheat		Crème Fraîche	Wild Boar, Pheasant)
		Butter	Pâté (Duck, Goose, Wild
		Ice Cream	Boar)
		Yogurt (Cow, Sheep, Goat)	Smoked Meats
		Quark	
		Cheese	

The Greenmarket Recipes

Vegetable Bouillon

Diane Forley

Chicken Stock

Bill Telepan

Roasted Bell Peppers

Basic Pie Crust

The Greenmarket Pantry

Stocks and Broths—one and the same, for our purposes—are called for in several recipes in this book. Here are two you will find useful.

DIANE FORLEY

Vegetable Bouillon

Chef-owner Diane Forley of Verbena Restaurant is quiet but firmly spoken. It's a pleasure to talk to her and get her take on her daily visits to the market. She or one of her staff can be seen pulling a red wagon—the same kind we pulled each other around in as kids—through the market, loading it up with produce. One day I pointed to her purchases and asked: "What is this going to become?" and she told me about her delicious vegetable bouillon. The bouillon can be served as a vegetable broth, or used as a fragrant stock in any recipe that calls for it.

1/4	cup plus 1 tablespoon olive oil
3	large onions, halved
3	celery ribs, coarsely chopped
2	leeks, trimmed, washed, and coarsely chopped
2	large parsnips or turnips, scrubbed and coarsely chopped
2	large carrots, scrubbed and coarsely chopped
1	fennel bulb, coarsely chopped, including fronds
1	large tomato, diced
	Salt

Makes 1 quart

Heat 1 tablespoon of the olive oil in a small sauté pan over high heat and cook the onions, flat side down, until blackened on one side, about 5 minutes. Remove from the heat.

In a large stockpot, heat the remaining olive oil over medium heat. Add the celery, leeks, parsnips, carrots, and fennel and cook until softened but not browned, about 20 minutes. (Be careful not to caramelize the vegetables, unless a darker color and sweeter taste are desired.)

Add the onions and the tomato, and cover the vegetables with 7 cups of water. Bring to a boil, reduce the heat, and simmer for 40 minutes. Season to taste with salt and strain through a colander lined with cheesecloth into a large bowl. To maximize the yield, let the cheesecloth hang over the bowl for several hours.

Chicken Stock

Chef Bill Telepan has given us a number of Greenmarket-based recipes in the pages that follow. Here is his all-purpose, very useful chicken stock.

5 to 6 pounds chicken bones, necks, and wing tips
4 quarts water
1 onion, quartered
1 carrot, quartered lengthwise
1 stalk celery, quartered lengthwise
1 garlic bulb, broken into cloves
2 sprigs thyme
2 sprigs parsley
1 teaspoon black peppercorns

Makes about 3 quarts

Place all of the ingredients in a stockpot and bring to a boil over medium heat. Reduce the heat and simmer gently, skimming frequently, for 6 hours. Let cool, strain, and refrigerate or freeze.

Roasted Bell Peppers

Bell peppers may be roasted in the broiler or over a stovetop gas burner.

Broiler Method: Preheat the broiler. Rub the peppers lightly with olive or vegetable oil and roast under the broiler, turning, until blackened on all sides.

Stovetop Method: Place the peppers directly on the burner, turning, until blackened.

After roasting, place the peppers in a paper bag for 5 minutes, or place in a bowl and cover with an inverted bowl for 5 minutes, then peel and seed.

Basic Piecrust

A successful piecrust needs only a few ingredients. This one, with no sugar, can be used for any single-crust sweet fruit pie, such as Ruth Reichl's Apricot Pie (see page 61) and Maury Rubin's Indian Apple Pie (see page 122).

1½   cups all-purpose flour
½   teaspoon salt
½   cup cold butter or shortening (or a combination), cut into half-tablespoon-size pieces
3   to 4 tablespoons ice water

Makes one 9-inch piecrust

In a large bowl, toss together the flour and salt. Add the butter and work into the flour with your fingertips until crumbly. Drizzle 3 tablespoons of the water on top and work into the flour mixture until it starts to clump together. If the mixture seems too dry, sprinkle with the remaining tablespoon of water. Work the dough lightly into a ball, kneading a couple of times to blend. Form into a disk, wrap, and refrigerate for 30 minutes.

On a lightly floured surface, roll out the dough to an 11-inch circle, dusting with flour as necessary. Roll the dough onto a rolling pin, then unroll onto a 9-inch pie pan, centering the dough and fitting it into the bottom. Trim, then roll the top edge under and crimp decoratively. Refrigerate uncovered for up to 1 hour until ready to fill.

Summer

After winter's gift of rest and spring's promise of renewal, here comes summer! Neighborhood markets everywhere come alive and the year-round farmers' tables at the Union Square Greenmarket fill with produce. As summer dawns, I think of all the farmers' markets across America as enormous empty canvases waiting to be painted. Shades of "snow-pea" green, "orangeglo" watermelon yellow, "zucchini-blossom" orange, "rainbow-trout" pink, and "howling-mob-corn" white will flow to the bare markets from farms bursting into bloom. When summer is in full swing, the markets will be a riot of color.

At the start of the season, our Greenmarket stalls offer rows of pink, purple, white, red, and yellow bedding flowers, both annuals and perennials, that are quickly snatched up by home gardeners and window-box enthusiasts. Tim and Jill Stark's tomatoes, appearing after July, alone could electrify the market with their vivid red, yellow, black, purple, peach, and pink; Kenneth Migliorelli's delicate green sugar snaps complement the mix. Fred Wilklow's glossy black-red cherries, red raspberries, and dark blackberries invite tasting, and Henry and Sue Smith's golden corn, piled high and tempting customers in droves, seems the very soul of summer.

Every season has its special joy, but for many of us, summer is what Greenmarket is all about. It means going out with an empty market basket and bringing home a staggering load every time. It encourages giving in to any whim, knowing that whatever we pick will look gorgeous on the grill, in the salad bowl, or on the fruit platter. How can you go wrong with sweet yellow or white corn, golden beets, lita squash, heirloom tomatoes, baby globe carrots, butterhead lettuce, radicchio, bok choy, juicy cherries, blueberries, peaches, plums, watermelon. What's for dinner tonight? I haven't a clue. I'm waiting for Greenmarket to surprise me!

Summer shopping makes for a great outing with the kids. Buy extra because most of it will be happily gobbled up on the walk or ride back home, or even in the course of your market tour. Countless pounds of cherries and sugar snaps never make it to the kitchen.

Filling Your Market Basket in Summer
July, August, September

Cut Flowers	Edible Garden Starters	Oregano	Gem Marigold
Wildflowers	Herbs	Thyme	Dianthus (Carnation; Pink)
Peony	Lettuce	Rosemary	Chive Blossom
Blue Globe Thistle		Cilantro	Zucchini Blossom
Lupine	Freshly Cut Herbs	Savory (Winter and Summer)	
Zinnia	French Tarragon	mer)	Lettuce
Salvia	Anise Hyssop	Lemon Verbena	Batavian or French
Sunflower	Chervil	Lemongrass	(Canasta)
Dahlia	Lemon Balm	Shiso (Beefsteak Leaves)	Butterhead or Bibb (Brune
Snapdragon	Bee Balm (Bergamot)		d'Hiver)
Tuberose	Basil	Edible Flowers	Crisphead or Iceberg
	Dill	Borage	(Chou de Naples)
Ornamental Garden Starters	English Black Peppermint	Rose	Cos or Romaine (Little
Bedding plants	Egyptian Peppermint	Lavender	Gem)

Looseleaf (Black Seeded Simpson)

Salad and Cooking Greens
Purslane
Baby Mustard
Arugula
Radicchio
Dandelion, Red or Green
Escarole
Lamb's Quarters
Shungiku (Edible Chrysanthemum)
Bok Choy
Swiss Chard

Vegetables
Sugar Snap Pea
English Pea (Shelling or Green Pea)
Cucumber
Summer Squash: Zucchini; Cocozelle (Marrow); Lita (Lebanese); Ronde de Nice; Yellow Crookneck; Cucuzzi (Bottle Gourd; Long Green); Tenerumi (Squash Runners)
Corn: Bi-color; White; Yellow
Eggplant: Bambino; Rosa Bianca; Kermit (Thai); Turkish Orange
Celery; Red Celery
Okra
Rhubarb
Beans, Shelling: Fava (Broad Bean); Lima; Cranberry; Soy (Edamame)

Beans, Snap: String; Pole; Bush
French Filet (*Haricot Vert*)
Fennel

Cultivated Mushrooms
Button
Cremini
Portobello
Shiitake

Wild Mushrooms
Hen of the Woods
Hedgehog (Pied de Mouton)
Honey
Porcini (Cèpe)
Puffball
Amethyst Deceiver
Horse Mushroom (Field)
Blewit

Root Crops
Beet: Red; White; Golden; Striped (*Chioggia* or Candy Cane)
Kohlrabi
Leek
Scallion
Carrot: Baby; Orange; Yellow; Belgian White; Red; Thumbelina
Shallot
New Potato
Ginseng
Bunching (Spring) Onion
Cilantro Root
Garlic (Rocambole or top-setting varieties)
Garlic Top

Onion: Red Torpedo; White Bermuda; Walla Walla; Sweet Flat Red

Fruit
Strawberry
Cherry
Blueberry
Wild Blueberry
Currant
Raspberry: Red; Purple; Black; Yellow
Gooseberry
Mulberry
Blackberry
Elderberry
Peach, Cling
Peach, Freestone: Jersey Queen; Stark Saturn (Flat or Doughnut Peach); Iron Mountain
Apricot
Nectarine
Melon: Cantaloupe; Muskmelon; Watermelon
Plum: President; Blue Damson; Green Gage; Mirabelle; Prune; Shiro; Elephant Heart; Methley

Peppers
Bell
Frying
Hot
Spice

Tomatoes
Beefsteak
Cherry (includes pear-shaped)

Currant
Plum
Husk (Cape Gooseberry, Poha, Ground Cherry)
Tomatillo (larger cousin of Husk)

Eggs
Chicken
Duck

Poultry, Meat, and Game
Guinea Hen
Pheasant (young)
Pekin Duck
Chicken
Rabbit

Fish and Seafood
Bluefish
Black-Backed Flounder
Sea Trout (Weakfish)
Spanish Mackerel
Lobster
Whelk (Conch)
Squid
Smoked Fish

Also available in summer
dried flowers; grains, such as cornmeal, buckwheat groats, rye, and wheat berries; honey; maple syrup; prepared products such as cider, cherry juice, and jams; and seasonal baked goods such as fruit pies, doughnuts, and muffins.

Summer

Summer Recipes

Roasted Red Bell Pepper Gazpacho
  Roger W. Straus
Duck Salad with Fresh Peas and Radishes
  Peter Ivy
Goat Cheese, Lentil, and Vegetable Salad
  Michael Romano
Heirloom Tomato Salad with Chiles and Feta
    Cheese
  Ilene Rosen
Sweet-Spiced Cape Gooseberry Chutney
  Michael Romano
Red and Green Fresh Vegetables with Pasta
  Flavia Bacarella
Sweet Pepper Sauce for Pasta
  Tim Stark
Coach Farm's Goat Cheese Gnocchi and Roasted
    Red Pepper-Tomato Sauce
  Bill Telepan
Radicchio Sauce for Pasta Shells
  George Deem
Roasted Corncakes Stuffed with Goat Cheese and
    Chives
  Judith Schiff
Braised Green Beans with Onions, Bacon, and
    Summer Savory (Bohnen Kraut)
  Gray Kunz
Roasted Succotash of Sweet Corn and Fava Beans
  Kevin Johnson
Sicilian Squash Tendrils (Tenerumi)
  Paula Wolfert

Long Green Italian Squash
  Margaret Ruta
Roasted Trout with Summer Vegetables
  Waldy Malouf
Scallops with Market Vegetable Sauce
  Michaela Kane Schaeffer
Braised Chicken with Sweet Red Peppers and
    Fennel
  Erica De Mane
Onion Lovers' Dip
  Tracey Seaman
Use-up-the-Fruit Pancake
  Peggy Kent
Apricot Pie
  Ruth Reichl
Mom's Cherry Pie
  Connie McCabe
Peach Coffee Cake
  Jim Fobel
Golden Watermelon Ice
  Melissa Clark
Cherry Soup with Black Mint and Lemon Sorbet
  Wayne Nish
Fresh Blackberry Ice Cream
  Tracey Seaman
Peach Jam
  Stephanie Teuwen

MARKET PEOPLE
Henry and Sue Smith

"Growing up on a sweet-corn farm I could never figure out why anyone would want to eat day-old corn," says Henry Smith of Sycamore Farms. "It made no sense to us. My dad would feed day-old corn to the hogs!"

Farmers who sell produce at roadside stands

Henry Smith

grow most of their own crops, but they often find that corn takes up too much land and they turn to others for their supply. Henry's dad started growing sweet corn to sell to local roadside stands in the mid-1960s, and after a few years, he was supplying many of the stands in Northern New Jersey, Rockland and Westchester counties, and Connecticut. Soon, his dad's farm was producing two hundred acres of sweet corn, along with one hundred acres of other crops.

The Smiths' Greenmarket customers like to se-

LIMA BEAN TIPS

Buying   When shopping for lima beans, remember that the fuller the pod, the better the bean. Don't be put off by rust spots on the pod; these blemishes won't affect the beans. You should be able to feel the beans inside the pod, but don't squeeze them!   ***Cooking***   The best way to cook lima beans, according to Alvina, is the simplest. Shell the beans and plunge them into boiling water until tender (about five minutes), drain, and toss in a little butter or olive oil. Sprinkle with salt, pepper, and chopped fresh herbs.

lect their own corn, and many shoppers prefer to husk the ears before taking them home. "A lot of them say, 'I have to husk the corn because I have a small apartment.'" Henry smiles, and his eyes twinkle as he thinks of asking them: "Small apartment? Does that mean you can only buy cherry tomatoes?"

MARKET PEOPLE
Alvina Frey

Alvina Frey, "the bean lady," sold her vegetables and plants at Greenmarket from 1976—when the market opened—to 1999. Now retired, she shares her wisdom with the younger farmers. She traces her green thumb to her grandmother, who, after coming to America from Germany with her husband, purchased the farm while working at the Paterson silk mills.

Alvina remembers her childhood: "I started helping on the farm as soon as I could walk. My first paid job was a contract job. I was seven years old and my father offered me ten dollars to weed a large field of corn—by hand, of course. When I figured it out, it came to precious little per hour. I got smart and by the time I was eight years old, I had contracted for a better wage.

"When I was sixteen years old it rained for forty-one days in the summer. We had to stand on boxes to pick the tomatoes, and the water was still over my ankles. We'd try to dry our clothes on the wood stove but they were just too soaked to dry.

Alvina Frey

"My father planted his crops in three cycles. This way he hoped to still have crops to harvest around Thanksgiving. We kids [Alvina, sister Elsie, and brother Frank] would pray for a killing frost, so the plants would die and we wouldn't have to pick any more."

Alvina loves beans—not just elegant legumes like *haricots verts,* but earthy limas, as well. I hated lima beans when I was a kid, but that was before I met Alvina. One day I was telling her how much I despised the chalky-tasting things, when she popped a freshly shelled plump one in my mouth and ordered : "Shut up and chew!" I did. I loved it. (Can you believe it?) The flavor was delicate, echoing the pale green color; the texture was like silk, not the mush I remembered. Today, I can't get enough of them, and neither can anyone else, it seems. Early on Wednesday and Saturday mornings, customers gathered under Frey's awning to pick through the beans she harvested the day before. Along side her blue van stood a line of large bean-filled bags destined for some of New York's finest restaurants.

MARKET PEOPLE
Rocco and Kenneth Migliorelli

It is a beautiful summer morning in 1939 and the rows of attached one- and two-family houses that make up the Italian neighborhoods of Wakefield and Williamsbridge in the Bronx are coming to life. In the distance, a voice can be heard crying out: "Farmaiolo! Farmaiolo!"—"The farmer!"—as a horse-drawn wagon, piled high with freshly picked vegetables, slowly comes into view, driven by Angelo Migliorelli

Kenneth Migliorelli and his son Sam

and his son, Rocco. They are selling produce grown on their farm, just as Migliorellis have done, in Italy and America, for more than one hundred years.

Today, Kenneth Migliorelli, the son of Rocco and grandson of Angelo, can be heard at the Union Square Greenmarket, calling out his modern version of "Farmaiolo!" "Sugar snaps! Sugar snaps! Who wants to try a free sugar snap?" Ken and Rocco's harvest of sugar snaps is packed in bushel baskets that Ken stacks side by side and one on top of another, as he builds his market display early on a summer morning. The sight of these bright, crisp pods brings passing commuters to a complete halt; it is enough to make them forget what time it is.

Tomatoes
The Red Tide

The tomato has had a long, delicious, and sometimes troubled history. Originating in South America, migrating north to Mexico, and sailing from there to Spain with returning Spanish adventurers, tomatoes spread across Europe and eventually made their way back to the Americas. For a long time they were considered poisonous, but by the late 1800s, they had become an accepted food. More recently, tomatoes have suffered at the hands of large commercial growers and the supermarkets they supply. Too many American shoppers know them only as bland, mealy, waxy globes—nothing like the glorious *pommes d'amour* of culinary poetry.

Contrast these with the displays of bright-colored, juicy, flavorful, farm-fresh tomatoes adorning Greenmarket—a tomato-lover's dream come true. Greenmarket farmers grow and sell 120 varieties,

TIPS

Tamara Holt, Food Editor of Redbook magazine Tamara's List of the World's Ten Easiest and Best Dishes No recipes are needed for these dishes. The pure fresh flavors of local seasonal market produce have the integrity to stand on their own and are best when unadorned and simply allowed to shine. Amounts are up to you.

* Sliced Tomatoes with Olive Oil and Salt
* Steamed Fresh Corn with Butter
* Toasted Bread with Goat Cheese and Basil
* Roasted Beets with Chervil
* Sautéed Spinach with Garlic
* Roasted Parsnips and Carrots
* Boiled New Potatoes with Butter and Salt
* Melon with Mint
* Peaches with Yogurt and Honey
* Strawberries and Cream

among them, Aunt Ruby's German Green, Banana Legs, Green Zebra, Mortgage Lifter, Purple Calabash, and Tangerine. The imaginative names of these jewels are surpassed only by their eye-catching colors, shapes, and sizes.

MARKET PEOPLE
Tim and Jill Stark

Eckerton Hill Farms offers an old-fashioned take on farming, steering clear of high technology and opting for purity. Every plant is set in the earth by hand, compost is carried by the workers up and down the hilly acres, no machines are used for harvesting, and smokers must walk a quarter mile from the fields to take a puff, then must wash their hands with bleach and alcohol. But when Tim kneels down to weed crops, his cell phone is at his ear. Here in rural Pennsylvania as it must have been a century ago, "Tomato Tim" is fielding telephone calls from New York City restaurants like The Four Seasons and promising to fill orders.

Tim grew up on the property where his farm now stands; when he was a child, his parents rented out the

Tim Stark

TOMATO TIP

Author, cooking instructor, and food historian Michael Krondl has this to say about buying tomatoes: "Buy them in staged ripeness, so you have one for each day." He prefers to eat them raw: "Things I get at Greenmarket are best left as untouched as possible. They're so good just the way you find them."

land to tenant farmers and orchardists. After he graduated from Princeton, he wrote, taught school, worked for New York City, and married Jill Rosenthal, a law student. (They are now the parents of Gwendolyn Rose, born March 26, 1998.) Then Tim returned to his roots, and began growing tomato and pepper seedlings under lights in his Brooklyn apartment.

Tim and Jill moved the young plants to the farm in Pennsylvania and, after a couple of years, moved themselves to Pennsylvania. He slowly began taking back the land that had been rented out for corn and grain and instead planted peppers, melons, and the crop he is famous for, heirloom tomatoes. In August 1998, Eckerton Hill Farms sold four thousand pounds of tomatoes at the Union Square Greenmarket alone.

Tomato Chart

For anyone accustomed to ordinary tomatoes—even home-grown beefsteaks—heirloom tomatoes will be a revelation. They are available in a variety of shapes, sizes, and colors, each with a distinctive aroma and flavor. Unlike the commonly available hybrids that often are bred for a long shelf life at the expense of quality, these come from seeds that have been passed down for centuries by farmers committed to preserving their unique characteristics. The tomatoes listed are grown by Tim Stark at Eckerton Hill Farms and by other farmers, and are available at the Union Square Greenmarket. Look for these varieties at your local markets, as well.

Names given to heirloom tomatoes by their growers can be idiosyncratic, to say the least, and difficult to trace. While the legend of Pink Mortgage Lifter is well known, both the mysterious Hugh's and Nicky Crain can be mighty hard to find.

Variety and Appearance	Taste and Texture	Let's Eat!
Aunt Ruby's German Green Pale green skin turns yellowish-pink when ripe; green flesh. Large, slightly flattened beefsteak seeds were saved from extinction by Ruby Arnold of Greeneville, Tennessee.	Meaty texture, sweet flavor with background hints of spice.	Use in sauces, soups, or sandwiches. An excellent tomato for pasta sauces.
Banana Legs Yellow, elongated mini-banana shape with pointed bottom.	Subtle taste, crunchy texture, though some consider it bland and mealy.	Used for tomato paste; good sliced in salads or on a mixed tomato platter.
Black Pear Dark red-black mahogany-like color; pear-shaped.	Rich, sweet flavor with background hints of Burgundy wine.	Best eaten right off the vine; delicious in salads. Don't cook this one!
Brandywine Deep-pink skin and flesh; large, classic beefsteak style. A favorite of backyard gardeners. Traced to an Amish community in Chester, Pennsylvania, 1885.	Excellent deep flavor and texture set the standard for beefsteaks.	Good in sandwiches and salads, and just eating sliced. A favorite for gazpacho.
Cherokee Purple Dusty-pink skin turns dark purple on its shoulders when ripe. Flattened globe shape; average weight is 10 ounces. Thought to have been grown over 100 years ago by the Cherokee Indians in Tennessee.	Very rich flavor with good balance of acidity and fruitiness.	A favorite for sandwiches.
German Red Strawberry Pink to crimson skin and flesh. Up to 3 inches long and ¾ pound.	Rich flavor and very meaty flesh.	Excellent for any fresh use: salads, sandwiches, tomato platters.
Green Zebra Greenish-orange skin with deep-green stripes; round, about 2 inches in diameter.	Tangy and sweet-tasting.	Delicious with fresh goat cheese, sliced into salads, and in salsa.

Variety and Appearance	Taste and Texture	Let's Eat!
Hugh's Yellow skin with a pink blush; very large beefsteak, up to 6 inches in diameter and more than 2 pounds. Can be traced to Madison County, Indiana.	Peachy sweet, very juicy.	Excellent for juice, in salsa, or in a light tomato sauce.
Marvel Striped Skin splashed with orange and yellow; reddish streaked flesh. Seeds have been traced to Oaxaca, Mexico.	A tomato lover's dream. Very intense, full-flavored, and meaty.	Get out the salt and eat this as soon as you get it home.
Nicky Crain Pink; large, may weigh up to 2 pounds each. Ox-heart shape (like an elongated valentine).	Sweet and meaty.	Use in sandwiches and salads, or even with flowers and herbs as a table decoration.
Peach Somewhat fuzzy pink or yellow skin; pink or yellow flesh; Ping-Pong–ball size.	Juicy rich flavor.	Eat out of hand or in salads.
Pink Mortgage Lifter During the 1940s, a West Virginia man developed this variety, sold the seedlings to his neighbors, and was able to pay off his mortgage. Very popular, large, dark-pink, with a flattened beefsteak shape.	Sweet flavor and a meaty texture. Has few seeds.	The king of sandwich tomatoes.
Purple Calabash Dark purple, somewhat ugly, with ruffled shoulders and dark, almost chocolate-colored patches. Similar-looking tomatoes were pictured in 16th-century herbals.	Juicy and flavorful, with red wine-like undertones.	Does not keep well, so use right away. Best for sauces, stewing, or sliced thick, drizzled with a little salt and olive oil, and topped with fresh mozzarella and basil.

Variety and Appearance	Taste and Texture	Let's Eat!
Striped German, also called **Old German.** Yellowish skin with red streaks; yellow flesh with a red center; large, beefsteak shape. Seeds have been traced back to Mennonite communities of Virginia.	Beautiful to behold and even better to eat.	Excellent for all fresh uses. Also good for light sauces.
Sun Gold Dark yellow-gold skin and flesh; cherry tomato.	Excellent flavor—better than candy.	Best eaten fresh and uncooked.
Tangerine Yellow; large, somewhat flattened.	Sweet, meaty, and super fruity taste.	Good in fresh soups (yellow gazpacho), salsas, coulis.
Yellow Bell Light yellow with a dull finish; plum-shaped.	Very meaty, sweet, flavor-packed.	Use for yellow tomato sauce, yellow ketchup.
Yellow Brandywine Looks like the *Tangerine*—sometimes it's hard to tell them apart.	Not as meaty as the *Tangerine*, but still very fruity.	Good in sandwiches and salads, but too watery for soups, sauces, or ketchup (requires a lot of cooking down).

MARKET PEOPLE
Ted and Susan Blew

In addition to its famous turnpike, sprawling suburbs, shopping malls, and universities, New Jersey has an abundance of beautiful farmland. Farmers Ted and Susan Blew and their four children—Charity, Eric, Amanda, and Jonathan—live in the central part of the state on a 160-acre farm that has been in continual production since 1865. In 1999 they raised more than 246 varieties of hot peppers and over 92 types of sweet, some of which had previously been grown only in tropical climates. These peppers appeal to the country's steadily growing appetite for Mexican, Szechuan, Indian, Thai, Indonesian, and other ethnic foods. The farm produces hull-less white popping corn and organic pork, as well.

Susan says: "My love afffair with peppers, both sweet and hot, can be traced to our Greenmarket customers. Many of our customers travel worldwide and bring back pepper seeds for me to grow. I also get tomato seeds. Chef Michael Romano of the Union Square Cafe always keeps me well supplied with seeds from Italy."

The Blews are fervent crusaders for organic farming. They believe that customers should ask restaurants: "What is the basis of the food you are serving me? Has this food been preserved, frozen, or treated with chemicals? How was it grown?" They stress that most people are concerned with the quality of the food they eat, but don't often ask the right questions.

Peppers

Peppers range from sweet bells, well known in salads, stuffing, and snacks, to incendiary Habaneros, a treat for the brave few. But don't avoid the unfamiliar! Peppers in all their variety offer a world of flavors that go way beyond their heat. Novices who want to reduce the heat of chile peppers are often advised to cut out the seeds, but that works only for older peppers; in the freshest peppers, like the ones you buy at

Joel Patraker's Not-So-Excellent Pepper Adventure

Years ago, I was visiting Ted and Susan Blew at their market stand with Chef Jamie Leeds, then executive sous chef at the Union Square Cafe. We were tasting samples of their ripe peppers—about twenty bite-size portions in all. Although the Habanero was not the last pepper I tried, my sample attached itself to me in the form of juice on my hand. Some dust blew into my eyes, and, unthinkingly, I raised my hand to brush it away. A few moments later I was cautioning a customer on the correct way to handle hot peppers, when my eyes began to itch. Within seconds they were tearing like open faucets and so inflamed that Jamie had to lead me by the hand to her restaurant kitchen for some industrial strength eyewash from the first-aid kit.

The Oak Grove stand

Greenmarket, the heat is in the veins, not the seeds. So get to know them slowly and gradually build your tolerance for their special intensity. Be prepared—a variety that is fairly mild in one batch may knock you for a loop in another. And handle them carefully, wearing rubber gloves, if necessary, because their heat-producing chemical, capsaicin, is a potent irritant of skin and eyes.

Like the tomato, the pepper is a fruit, not a vegetable; the part you eat is the edible reproductive body of a seed plant. The genus *Capsicum* includes all peppers, from the mildest to the hottest.

Native to South America—they originated in central Bolivia—peppers are perennials that are grown as annuals in colder climates. When grown in the northeastern United States, they require temperatures from the upper nineties to just over one hundred degrees and a very dry summer to produce exceptionally hot fruit. Cool, damp summers will result in milder peppers.

Pepper Chart

The organically grown peppers listed below are beautiful in their purity and electric in their flavors. They are sold fresh at farmers' markets; freeze or dry them whole during the summer months to help you get through cold winter nights. You can dry them on their branches for decorative use, then pick off the dried peppers when it's time to cook. But don't rub your eyes!

Although many of these peppers have traditionally been used in the cuisines of South and Central America, Asia, and the Caribbean, they are adaptable to the things we cook here and now, and they enhance

Susan Blew's Pepper Lore

* Habanero is Spanish for "from Havana"; Yucatán had major commercial ties with Cuba until the twentieth century. The Habanero is the only pepper cultivar in the Yucatán Peninsula that has no Mayan name.
* A pepper high can be just like a runner's high!
* Hot peppers are used medicinally for treating shingles and arthritis.
* Many Greenmarket customers handle peppers with plastic gloves or bags. Some people are so sensitive that their skin will blister at the touch of a pepper! When rinsing and cutting hot peppers, always wear gloves. (Twice, Susan didn't follow her own advice, and suffered severe blistering that lasted for twelve hours. Soaking her hands in bleach, vinegar, and milk didn't cool them, and she ended up immersing them in ice water until they felt numb.)
* Build up your body's immunity to the heat of hot peppers. Start with a mild variety and work your way up to the Habanero Red Savina—very slowly! This could take weeks or even months.
* If a pepper is too hot for your taste, just remove the veins (and the seeds if it is less than fresh) before eating it raw or cooking with it.

many other Greenmarket ingredients. I would rather experience each pepper anew and use it spontaneously in my favorite kinds of dishes, than be bound by custom. What a great way to expand your culinary horizons!

On the heat scale below, developed by Susan and Joel, peppers are rated from 0 to 10 in ascending order of fire. A sweet Corno di Toro would rate 0 while a Habanero Red Savina, one of the hottest peppers ever measured, would be off the chart at a searing 10+++.

Farmer Susan Blew's Favorite Peppers

Variety and Appearance	Heat (from 0 to 10)	Let's Eat!
Ají Amarillo *(fresh)*; **Cusqueño** *(dried)* Native to Peru. Green when unripe, yellow-orange to pure yellow when ripe; about ¾ inch wide and 3 inches long, with tapered ends.	8+ Very hot but with well-rounded flavor.	Adds zip to salsa. The *cusqueño* is the principal condiment for Peruvian foods, especially soups and stews.
Puca Uchu, Ají Riojo *(fresh)*; **Cusqueño** *(dried)* Native to Peru. Greenish-yellow when immature, red when fully ripe; tapers to a point and is longer and narrower than *Ají Amarillo*.	7+ Unusual spicy flavor, warm background taste.	Same as *Ají Amarillo*.
Ají Panca *(fresh)*; **Cusqueño** *(dried)* Native to Peru. Blackish-purple when immature, deep red when ripe; about 5 inches long, 1 inch across the top, and tapered.	5+ Spicy with hints of fruit.	Good for flavoring fish, vegetables, and poultry; same as *Ají Amarillo*.
Anaheim, often called **Long Green** Dull green when harvested for roasting; red when ripe; up to 8 inches long, 1½ inches across. *New Mexico* (smaller, more flavorful) and *Sandia* (very hot when ripe) are other varieties.	4.5–6 Mild to bland when green; roasting brings out flavor and lessens heat.	*Green:* Top of the line for roasting and chiles rellenos; good in chili or stews. Roadside stands in New Mexico roast freshly harvested *Anaheims* and customers can freeze them until needed. *Red:* good for stuffing; add a nice twist to scrambled eggs; dried are popular for *ristras* (strings of dried peppers). Dried and ground are used in chili powder and paprika.
Cascabella Spanish for "beautiful skin." Deep orange-red when ripe; ½-inch long, heart shaped.	8 Medium heat; warm flavor.	Use fresh, pickled, or dried. Good in sauces.

Variety and Appearance	Heat (from 0 to 10)	Let's Eat!
Cayenne Named for Cayenne River in French Guyana. Grown in Louisiana, Japan, India, Africa, and Mexico. Green, red, yellow, or golden; 2 to 7 inches long; pencil-thin cylinders or curvy crescents, both with tapered bottoms.	6–9 The hotter the growing season, the hotter the pepper. Bright, spicy flavor.	Use fresh or dried. Good for sauces, gumbos, shrimp and crayfish dishes.
Chilaca (fresh) seldom seen; **Pasilla (dried)** Shiny, reddish brown to chocolate black when ripe; 5 to 7 inches long; up to 1 inch across the top. *Pasilla* is wrinkled and the color of a raisin. (*pasa* is raisin in Spanish).	5+ Rich, smoky flavor with hints of chocolate that increase when the pepper is dried.	*Pasilla* is traditionally used in Mexican mole sauce; added to stews, and used with broiled fish and chicken.
Chimayo Named for New Mexican town of origin. Green when immature; red when ripe. Up to 6 inches long; slightly curved with flattened end.	5+ green 7+ red Mild, warm flavor when green; flavor and heat increase as it ripens.	*Green* used for stuffing; flavoring egg dishes. *Red* is used dried; a popular choice for *ristras* (strings of dried peppers).
Corno di Toro Red and yellow varieties. Named "horn of the bull" because of its shape; wide at the top, tapering and twisting to a point; up to 10 inches long.	0 Exceptionally sweet but balanced flavor, with subtle, spicy background flavor.	Popular Italian frying pepper. Good fresh, eaten out of hand, in a salad, or as crudité. Use in salsa along with hotter peppers. Can be roasted, then marinated, covered with olive oil, and frozen. The Blews' favorite sweet pepper.
Habanero Tan-orange or chocolate-mahogany; boxy; heart shaped, with protruding nipple on the bottom; about 2 inches long. **Habanero Red Savina** is the color of glossy red lipstick.	10+++ Unmistakable flavor and aroma, blend of tropical fruits and flowers, plus inner warmth. *Red Savina* is one of the hottest chiles ever measured, at 577,000 Scoville heat units.	Approach with caution; use sparingly, unless you are used to them. Add zip to sauces and stews; excellent with grilled fish, pork, or poultry. The Blews like this pepper, but warn that it is dangerous!

Jalapeño (fresh); Chipotle (dried and smoked) Best-known hot pepper; originated in Jalapa, Mexico. Dark green; about 2 inches long, stubby.

1 to 8
Heat depends upon variety. *Jalapeños'* heat is stronger than their flavor; *Chipotles* have a warm, smoky flavor.

Probably the most versatile hot pepper. Susan Blew loves it! Fresh *jalapeños* are used in vegetable or meat dishes, salsas, salads, and sauces. Can be stuffed. Also available canned or pickled. *Chipotles* are used in sauces, vinaigrettes, and soups.

Long Gold Hawaiian Habanero Seeds brought from Hawaii by Joel Patraker. Vibrant yellow; 2½ to 3 inches long by ¾ inch wide; tapered. **Long Red Hawaiian** is almost identical.

10++
Very hot, with exceptional, balanced flavor.

Use the same way, and with similar caution, as any other *Habanero*. Delicious with mashed potatoes.

Peter Pepper Soft green, red, or yellow varieties; 3 to 5 inches long, with skin folding into itself at the tip. Its shape makes it an interesting conversation piece—Susan Blew enjoys her customers' reactions when they look at it.

8+
Hot and pungent with a little acidic bite.

Can be pickled, dried, frozen, or used fresh.

Poblano (fresh); Ancho and Mulato (dried) *Poblano* is green when immature and red when ripe; *Ancho* is reddish brown; *Mulato* is blackish brown. Over 5 inches long and 3½ inches across the top, tapering slightly at the bottom.

4+–8
Meaty flesh is spicy with herbal and aromatic background flavors. *Poblanos'* heat levels vary greatly from farm to farm.

Poblanos are used for chiles rellenos and are excellent raw or cooked. Remove skin before using. *Anchos* are excellent in cooked dishes; used for chili powder, coloring agents. *Mulatos* have tough skin, sweet flavor. Used in cooked sauces; sold in paste form as pisado chile.

Scotch Bonnet Bright red, yellow, or chocolate; about ¾ inch across and a little over 1 inch long. Resembles a little tam o' shanter. Often mistaken for the equally hot but less aggressively flavored Habanero.

9–10+
Warning! Danger! Alluring, warm, and fruity bouquet can be quickly displaced by its extreme heat.

Popular throughout Caribbean countries as a key ingredient in hot sauces. Use sparingly in any fresh or cooked dish.

Variety and Appearance	Heat (from 0 to 10)	Let's Eat!
Serrano Originated in the Mexican mountain ridges (*serranías*) north of Puebla and Hidalgo. Bright red when mature; 2 to 2½ inches long, tapered to a blunt point.	9+ Delicious pepper flavor. Susan warns of "branding-iron heat."	Can be eaten raw, roasted, pickled, or dried. Use in salsas, guacamole, sauces, chili.
Tepin (Bird Pepper) Bright red; tiny, round fruit. Grown from wild seed; hard to find. Historically were eaten by birds who then spread the seeds via their droppings.	8++ Balanced hints of spice and fruit, pleasingly warm. Heat level increases when dried. An amazing wallop for a pepper this size.	Perfect for spicing up fish and chicken dishes, jellies, sauces. Easy to dry at home; use in place of crushed red pepper.
Yatasufusa (Chile Japones) Red with orange overtones; about 4 inches long; narrow, straight body tapers to a stubby point.	8++ Fiery hot; very rich, intense flavor.	Very popular in Japan; in the U.S., found mostly at farmers' markets and specialty stores. Perfect for all fresh and cooked preparations. Dried and ground used as a seasoning.

Lettuce

Greenmarket, and your farmers' market, offer lettuce in all its magnificent variety. Here are a few exceptional examples:

Batavian or French are in a class by themselves. They are a combination of looseleaf and crisphead lettuces, blending sweet flavor with crisp and juicy texture. Traditionally seen in French farmers' markets, they are gaining in popularity with American growers and consumers.

Butterhead or Bibb are easily identified by their small, round heads and loosely packed leaves, which are very tender and have a butterlike taste and texture.

Crisphead or Iceberg are distinguished by their crisp leaves and tightly wrapped heads. Many shoppers equate them with tasteless supermarket icebergs—a big mistake. At market, the leaves have a mildly sweet background flavor.

Cos or Romaine are richly flavored. They have long, broad leaves, tender at the top and thicker, crisp, and juicy toward the bottom.

Looseleaf are nonheading, resembling a circular bouquet of leaves gathered together at the base. Their leaf types are the most diverse of all lettuces, including smooth, frilly, curled, and ruffled with splashes of color (from bronze tips to solid burgundy). They have mild flavor and soft, creamy texture.

Roasted Red Bell Pepper Gazpacho

Roger W. Straus, president and CEO of the venerable publishing firm of Farrar, Straus & Giroux, is a regular market customer who often buys roses from Marry at Michael Barry's flower stand. Over time, Marry told him of her interest in photography, and she presented him with a beautiful portrait that she'd taken of him.

Roasted bell peppers give a delicious twist to this classic summer soup.

FOR THE GAZPACHO

- 4 large red bell peppers, roasted and peeled (see page 15)
- 2 garlic cloves, crushed or minced
- 2 to 3 cups tomato juice (or mixed vegetable juice)
- 2 tablespoons olive oil
- 1 tablespoon red wine vinegar
- 1 tablespoon balsamic vinegar
- Pinch of cayenne
- Salt and freshly ground pepper

Makes 4 1/3 cups

Puree the bell peppers and garlic in a blender, adding tomato juice until the desired consistency is obtained. With the motor running, add the olive oil, vinegar, cayenne, and salt and pepper to taste. Chill for several hours or overnight.

FOR THE GARNISH

- 2 Kirby cucumbers, peeled, seeded, and finely diced
- 1 small green bell pepper, stemmed, seeded, and finely diced
- 1/4 cup finely diced sweet onion
- 1 large tomato, seeded and finely diced
- 1 jalapeño pepper, seeded and finely diced
- Pinch of cayenne, optional

For the garnish, combine all the vegetables and add the cayenne if desired.

To serve, divide the gazpacho among 4 soup bowls and sprinkle with the vegetable garnish.

PETER IVY

Duck Salad with Fresh Peas and Radishes

This dish from a most creative chef combines duck with fresh seasonal ingredients as well as complex Asian flavors, and it is pleasing, savory, and rich.

FOR THE DUCK

6	Long Island or Pekin duck legs
$1/4$	cup dark soy sauce
$1/4$	cup honey
	1-inch-long piece fresh ginger, finely chopped
3	cloves garlic, minced
2	tablespoons dark sesame oil
$1/2$	cup white wine
$1/2$	teaspoon Chinese five-spice powder
$1/2$	jalapeño pepper, minced

Makes 6 servings

In a large bowl, combine the duck legs, soy sauce, honey, chopped ginger, garlic, sesame oil, wine, five-spice powder, and jalapeño. Refrigerate for 4 hours or overnight.

Preheat the oven to 400°F.

Place the duck legs in a large roasting pan. Pierce the skin all over with a two-prong fork and roast, turning occasionally, until the duck is fully cooked and nicely browned. Remove and allow to cool. Remove the bones and cut the meat into bite-size chunks.

3 tablespoons rice vinegar

1 tablespoon plus 1 teaspoon honey

1 teaspoon soy sauce

1 teaspoon dark sesame oil

¼ teaspoon salt

Freshly ground pepper

¼ cup vegetable oil

1 cup shelled fresh peas (from 1 pound pea pods)

⅓ pound mesclun greens (8 cups, lightly packed)

¼ pound pea shoots (6 cups, lightly packed)

10 radishes, thinly sliced

¼ cup finely chopped fresh cilantro

3 scallions, thinly sliced

For the salad dressing, whisk together in a small bowl the vinegar, honey, soy sauce, sesame oil, salt, and pepper to taste. Gradually whisk in the oil in a fine stream.

In a small saucepan, cook the peas in lightly salted boiling water until tender, 8 to 10 minutes.

To serve, toss the duck with ¼ cup of the dressing and set aside. In a large bowl, toss the mesclun, pea shoots, radishes, and peas with the remaining dressing.

Divide among 6 dinner plates. Place some of the duck on top of each portion, and scatter cilantro and scallions on top.

MICHAEL ROMANO

Goat Cheese, Lentil, and Vegetable Salad

Chef Michael Romano of the Union Square Cafe offers this attractive, market-fresh salad, with crisp-cooked vegetables enhanced by tart goat cheese and hearty lentils.

A tip from the chef: rubbing off the beet skin after cooking, instead of peeling it with a knife, allows the vegetable to keep its natural shape, so you'll end up with attractive, round slices.

FOR THE VINAIGRETTE

6	tablespoons walnut oil
2	tablespoons French red wine vinegar
1	teaspoon raspberry vinegar
1	teaspoon Dijon mustard
1/2	teaspoon salt
	Freshly ground black pepper

Makes 4 servings

Combine the vinaigrette ingredients in a jar. Close the lid tightly and shake vigorously.

FOR THE SALAD

2	medium beets, unpeeled, roots trimmed to 1/2 inch
1 1/2	teaspoons kosher salt
1/2	pound *haricots verts*
10	ounces (1 log) fresh goat cheese (preferably Coach Farm)
1/2	tablespoon tarragon
1/2	tablespoon chervil
1/2	tablespoon parsley
1/2	tablespoon chopped chives
1/8	teaspoon freshly ground black pepper
1/8	teaspoon minced garlic
1/4	teaspoon fresh lemon juice
2	tablespoons extra virgin olive oil
1	head frisée, washed and trimmed
1	cup cooked brown or green lentils

In a small saucepan, cover the beets with cold water, add ½ teaspoon of the salt, and bring to a boil. Reduce the heat and simmer until a knife pierces the beets easily, about ½ hour. When the beets are cool enough to handle, trim the ends and gently rub off their skins with a paper towel. Cut the beets in half and then into ¼-inch slices, and set aside.

Bring 1½ quarts of water to a boil and add ½ teaspoon of the salt. Cook the *haricots verts* until they are crisp-tender, about 4 minutes. Drain and refresh in ice water. Drain and set aside.

To prepare the goat cheese, combine the cheese, herbs, remaining ½ teaspoon salt, pepper, garlic, and lemon juice in the bowl of a kitchen mixer. Whip the cheese until it becomes light and airy, 4 to 5 minutes. Slowly drizzle in the olive oil and taste for seasoning. Set aside.

To assemble the salad, toss the frisée with some of the salad dressing and arrange on 4 plates. Lightly drizzle the beets and *haricots verts* with more of the vinaigrette and arrange atop the frisée, leaving room in the center for the cheese. In a bowl, toss the cooked lentils with the remaining vinaigrette. Season with additional salt and pepper, if desired.

Place a 2½ by 1¼-inch ring mold in the center of one plate of frisée and spoon one quarter of the lentils into the mold, pressing lighly to pack them down. Spoon one quarter of the goat cheese mixture onto the lentils and smooth down with the back of a spoon. Gently lift the ring mold. Repeat with the 3 remaining plates. Serve.

Dana Cowin, editor in chief of *Food & Wine* magazine

ILENE ROSEN

Heirloom Tomato Salad with Chiles and Feta Cheese

With The City Bakery just a stone's throw from Greenmarket, Chef de Cuisine Ilene Rosen can find gorgeous heirloom tomatoes, available through the summer. She adds the savory accent of fresh feta cheese and the electricity of chiles. The more varieties of tomatoes you use, the more colorful and interesting your salad will be.

3	pounds heirloom tomatoes (such as Cherokee Purple, Banana Legs, Black Pear, Hugh's, Green Zebra, Peach), sliced
1	pint mixed-variety cherry tomatoes, halved
1/2	pint currant tomatoes, stems left on
4	Ají peppers, stems removed (use a mild Ají)
1/2	cup canola oil
	Kosher salt
1/3	pound (or to taste), sheep's milk feta cheese, crumbled
10	leaves purple basil, slivered

Makes 6 servings

Ilene Rosen

Arrange the heirloom, cherry, and currant tomatoes on a platter. Puree the peppers and canola oil in a food processor or blender and season to taste with salt. Drizzle over the tomatoes and sprinkle with the feta cheese and basil leaves.

MICHAEL ROMANO
Sweet-Spiced Cape Gooseberry Chutney

Cape gooseberries are not berries, but are tomato-like fruits in the tomatillo family, with a mild pineapple-like flavor. They are golden yellow, the size of marbles, and wrapped in papery husks. Michael Romano, executive chef of Union Square Cafe, likes to combine them with fragrant Indian spices to make a winning chutney.

2$\frac{1}{2}$	tablespoons coriander seeds
1	teaspoon green cardamom seeds
1$\frac{1}{2}$	teaspoons turmeric
2	tablespoons vegetable oil
1$\frac{1}{2}$	tablespoons mustard seeds
6	celery stalks, minced
1	medium onion, minced
1	teaspoon minced ginger
2	cups sugar
1	cup apple cider vinegar
1	cup pineapple juice
3	pounds cape gooseberries, husks removed
	Zest of 1 lemon, finely minced
	Zest of 1 orange, finely minced
3	jalapeño peppers, chopped (2 seeded and 1 with seeds)
	Kosher salt and freshly ground pepper

Makes 10 servings

Grind the coriander and cardamom seeds to a fine powder in a spice grinder. Transfer to a small bowl; add the turmeric and enough water to make a paste.

Heat the oil in a large, deep skillet over medium heat. Add the mustard seeds and shake the pan while the seeds "pop" and darken. Add the spice paste and cook 3 to 4 minutes, stirring constantly.

Add the celery, onion, ginger, and $\frac{1}{4}$ cup water to the pan, cover, and cook, stirring occasionally, to soften but not brown the vegetables, 4 to 5 minutes. Stir in the sugar and allow it to melt. Add the cider vinegar, pineapple juice, and Cape gooseberries and return to a boil. Lower the heat and simmer the fruit until it is very tender, about 25 minutes. Stir in the lemon and orange zests and the jalapeños, season with salt and pepper to taste, and cook, uncovered, an additional 5 minutes. Serve at room temperature. The chutney can be refrigerated in a tightly closed container for up to 1 week.

FLAVIA BACARELLA

Red and Green Fresh Vegetables with Pasta

Flavia Bacarella and Keith Stewart own Keith's Organic Farm in Westtown, New York, where Flavia, a talented painter, works in a studio that looks out over the lush fields. This colorful dish, combining raw and cooked ingredients, is a reflection of Flavia's artistic sense of season. She prepared it for me at the farm with ingredients that had been picked minutes before.

FOR THE RAW VEGETABLES

- 3 pounds large ripe tomatoes, coarsely chopped
- 1 red bell pepper, seeded and diced
- 6 garlic cloves, smashed or finely sliced
- 1/2 cup finely chopped flat-leaf parsley
- 1/2 cup finely chopped basil

Makes 4 servings

FOR THE STEAMED VEGETABLES

- 1/2 pound Swiss chard, washed and chopped into small pieces
- 1/2 pound broccoli rabe, washed and chopped into small pieces
- 1 pound sugar snap peas or snow peas, stringed

TO ASSEMBLE

- 1 pound farfalle or penne pasta
- 1/4 cup olive oil
- 2 tablespoons balsamic vinegar
- 1 teaspoon kosher salt
- 1/2 teaspoon freshly ground pepper
- 1 large zucchini, grated
- Freshly grated or shaved Parmesan cheese

Place all the raw vegetables in a large pasta bowl.

In a vegetable steamer, steam the Swiss chard, the broccoli rabe, and the sugar snap peas. Steam until tender, about 5 minutes. Add to the raw vegetables in the pasta bowl.

Bring 4 quarts of salted water to a boil in a large pot and cook the pasta al dente. Drain and add to the bowl with the vegetables. Toss with the olive oil and balsamic vinegar and season with salt and pepper. Garnish with the grated zucchini and Parmesan.

TIM STARK
Sweet Pepper Sauce for Pasta

"Tomato Tim" Stark created this fresh sauce, using the good sweet onions, peppers, and tomatoes that he grows on his Eckerton Hill Farm in Pennsylvania. Have fun with the colors, and combine them at will, because aesthetics are as important as taste.

Try sprinkling some aged goat cheese on each portion. Delicious!

2	tablespoons olive oil
4	garlic cloves, smashed
1	medium sweet onion, coarsely chopped
3	large bell peppers (red, yellow, orange, or chocolate), stemmed, seeded, and coarsely chopped
1½	pounds (8 to 10) small tomatoes (Red Roma, Yellow Bell, Orange Banana, or Black Plum, to match bell pepper color), peeled and coarsely chopped
¾	teaspoon salt
1	pound pasta, your favorite variety
½	cup finely chopped basil leaves
	Salt and freshly ground pepper

Makes 4 to 6 servings

Heat the olive oil in a large skillet over medium heat. Add the garlic and cook, stirring, for 1 minute. Add the onion and cook until translucent, about 7 minutes. Add the bell peppers and cook until they begin to blister. Add the tomatoes and simmer until tender, about 20 minutes.

Pulse the pepper mixture in a food processor until coarsely chopped, return to the skillet, and keep warm until the pasta is ready.

Meanwhile, bring a large pot of salted water to a boil. Add the pasta and cook until al dente. Drain well in a colander.

In a large serving bowl, toss together the pasta, sauce, and basil. Season with salt and pepper.

BILL TELEPAN
Coach Farm's Goat Cheese Gnocchi and Roasted Red Pepper-Tomato Sauce

Goat cheese makes JUdson Grill Chef Bill Telepan's gnocchi tangy and delicate. Sauce them with the garden-fresh flavors of bell pepper, tomato, onion, and garlic, for a perfect Greenmarket dish.

FOR THE ROASTED RED PEPPER-TOMATO SAUCE

- 2 tablespoons olive oil
- 1/4 onion, coarsely chopped
- 1 garlic clove, smashed
- 1 cup coarsely chopped ripe tomato
- 1 cup vegetable stock, chicken stock, or water
- 1 red bell pepper, roasted (see page 15)
- 1/2 teaspoon salt
- 1/4 teaspoon freshly ground pepper

Makes 4 servings

Heat the oil in a skillet over medium heat. Add the onion and garlic and cook, stirring often, until tender but not colored, about 8 minutes. Add the tomato and stock, bring to a boil, and simmer 30 minutes. Add the pepper.

Puree in a food processor or blender, strain into a bowl, and season with salt and pepper. Can be made to this point up to 1 day ahead. Let cool, cover, and refrigerate. Rewarm before serving.

FOR THE GOAT CHEESE GNOCCHI

8	ounces Coach Farm goat cheese
2	large eggs, lightly beaten
1/2	teaspoon salt
1/4	teaspoon freshly ground black pepper
3/4	cup all-purpose flour
	Roasted red pepper-tomato sauce
1/4	cup grated Coach Farm aged goat cheese, for garnish
1/4	cup slivered fresh basil, for serving, plus leaves, for garnish

Bill Telepan

In a large bowl, combine the cheese, eggs, salt, and pepper, and mix well. Add the flour and mix just to combine—do not overwork.

On a lightly floured surface, roll out the dough ½ inch thick and cut into 1 by ½-inch pieces.

Bring a large pot of lightly salted water to a boil and add the gnocchi. When the water returns to a boil and all the gnocchi float to the top, cook for 2 minutes, then drain. Place the sauce in individual bowls or in a large serving bowl and top with the gnocchi. Garnish with the grated cheese and fresh basil.

Radicchio Sauce for Pasta Shells

George Deem, a steady market customer, was happy to share this recipe with Marry. Radicchio is a cross between a light cabbage and a thick lettuce that is usually eaten raw but holds up well in a sauce. This slightly bitter green has nuttiness and bite, and it makes a sauce that is delicious over pasta or, as we have found at home, over flounder or any light fish.

1	pound pasta shells
2	tablespoons extra virgin olive oil
2	medium garlic cloves, coarsely chopped
1	head radicchio, quartered, cored, and coarsely chopped
2	tomatoes cut into $1/2$-inch dice (peeled if desired)
5	tablespoons balsamic vinegar
12	oil-cured black olives, pitted and coarsely chopped
2	scallions, thinly sliced
$1/2$	teaspoon salt
$1/2$	teaspoon freshly ground black pepper
	Freshly grated or shaved Parmesan cheese, for serving

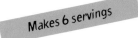

Makes 6 servings

Cook the pasta in a large pot of boiling salted water according to the package directions. Drain, and keep warm in a large bowl.

While the pasta is cooking, heat the oil in a large skillet over medium-high heat and add the garlic. Stir for 4 to 5 seconds, but do not brown. Add the radicchio and tomato and stir for 1 minute. Reduce the heat to low and add the vinegar. Continue cooking for 5 minutes, stirring occasionally, until the radicchio is softened.

Stir in the olives and scallions. Remove from the heat and season with the salt and pepper.

Add the sauce to the bowl of pasta and toss well. Serve the Parmesan cheese on the side.

JUDITH SCHIFF
Roasted Corncakes Stuffed with Goat Cheese and Chives

Judith Schiff, chef-owner of the restaurant Ready to Eat, is often seen pedaling her bicycle through the Green-markets. She has given me this unique summer recipe, a treat to serve at a barbecue or summer picnic, or even at an informal meal in a city apartment.

3	tablespoons corn oil
$1/2$	teaspoon salt
$1/2$	teaspoon freshly ground pepper
$1/4$	teaspoon paprika
4	ears fresh corn, shucked
2	large eggs
$1/2$	cup all-purpose flour
$1/4$	cup whole milk
$1/2$	teaspoon baking soda
$1/4$	cup minced fresh chives
6	ounces fresh goat cheese
2	tablespoons clarified butter or a combination of butter and oil
1	ripe red tomato, diced
1	ripe yellow tomato, diced
2	tablespoons slivered basil

Makes eight 3-inch pancakes, (4 appetizer or side-dish servings)

TIP

To clarify butter, melt it over low heat and simmer for a few minutes. Pour off and use the clear yellow portion; discard the solids. Butter will lose about $1/4$ of its original volume when treated this way, so measure accordingly.

Preheat an outdoor or stovetop grill.

Combine the oil with $1/4$ teaspoon of the salt, $1/4$ teaspoon of the pepper, and paprika. Rub the corn with the oil and roast until tender, about 10 minutes. Scrape the kernels into a bowl (there should be about $1\frac{1}{2}$ cups) and let cool completely.

In a large bowl, whisk together the eggs, flour, milk, baking soda, and the remaining salt and pepper until smooth, and add the corn. Let stand for 1 hour.

In a small bowl, mix together the chopped chives and the goat cheese.

Heat the clarified butter in a large nonstick skillet over medium-high heat and ladle a scant $1/4$ cup of the battter into the pan for each corncake; gently spread with the back of a spatula (this is important for even cooking). Crumble a teaspoon of the chive-cheese mixture in the center. Cover with another $1/4$ cup of batter, wait 10 seconds, flip, and cook until set on the other side. The cakes may be kept warm on a baking sheet in a low oven.

Divide the corncakes among 4 plates and top with the tomato and basil.

Braised Green Beans with Onions, Bacon, and Summer Savory (Bohnen Kraut)

Chef Gray Kunz and I were walking through Greenmarket one summer morning when he stopped at an inviting display of fresh herbs and picked up a bunch of summer savory. Savory and green beans are an excellent combination, he told me, so popular that home gardeners in Austria and Germany traditionally interplant the two.

8	slices bacon, cut into strips
1	medium white onion, finely chopped
2	pounds green beans or small *haricots verts*
¼	cup white wine
¼	cup stock (preferably vegetable stock)
1	bay leaf
2	cloves
1	ounce summer savory, tied into a bundle

Makes 4 main-course or 8 side-dish servings

Gray Kunz

In a deep skillet over medium heat, cook the bacon, turning occasionally, until crisp; transfer with tongs to paper towels. Add the onion to the pan and cook, stirring and scraping the pan, until golden, about 5 minutes. Add the green beans and turn to coat.

Pour in the white wine and stock. Stir in the bay leaf, cloves, and savory. Cover and simmer until the beans are tender, about 10 minutes.

Remove the savory, bay leaf, and cloves. Crumble the bacon on top and serve.

KEVIN JOHNSON

Roasted Succotash of Sweet Corn and Fava Beans

Chef Kevin Johnson's succotash is chunky and substantial, with charred vegetables and flavorful broth. Cooking the vegetables in a hot pan without any oil makes them taste almost as if they had been grilled and adds complexity to this classic American dish. Try zapping it with a bit of hot sauce.

1	cup shelled fava beans
1 1/2	cups fresh corn kernels (cut from 3 ears)
1	small red bell pepper, trimmed, seeded, and finely diced
1	small onion, finely diced
1	teaspoon ground cumin
1	small yellow squash, finely diced
1 1/2	tablespoons olive oil
2	garlic cloves, minced
1/2	cup vegetable broth
1/4	cup finely chopped cilantro
1/2	teaspoon salt
1/8	teaspoon freshly ground pepper

Makes 5 servings

Blanch the fava beans in a large pot of boiling, lightly salted water for about 2 minutes, remove to a bowl of ice water, and drain.

Place a large nonstick skillet over high heat. Add the corn kernels, bell pepper, onion, and cumin and cook, stirring occasionally, until the vegetables are slightly blackened, about 5 minutes. Add the squash, olive oil, and garlic, reduce the heat to medium, and stir for 1 minute. Stir in the broth, cilantro, salt, pepper, and blanched fava beans, and cook until the vegetables are thoroughly heated and the juices are mostly reduced, about 2 minutes.

PAULA WOLFERT

Sicilian Squash Tendrils (Tenerumi)

Paula Wolfert, the renowned food writer and scholar, discovered tenerumi, *the tendrils of long green Italian squash, on a trip to Sicily. When she was on Cape Cod, writing one of her recent cookbooks, she wanted to prepare some but couldn't find any locally, so she contacted me. It took three FedEx shipments, but we finally got the tendrils to her. She tells us: "Only at the Union Square Greenmarket in New York will you find them!"*

Tenerumi, *which means "rags," looks like a mass of green pasta with yellow flowers. Ms. Wolfert says that in this dish she "was at last able to appreciate the soft, velvety texture of* tenerumi." *She advises serving it at room temperature drizzled with good olive oil; as a dip for bread; or alongside veal, poultry, or fish. For more about long green Italian squash, see Margaret Ruta's recipe, following.*

1½   tablespoons olive oil, preferably extra virgin
1   onion, finely diced
2   large tomatoes, peeled, seeded, and finely diced
2   pounds *tenerumi* (buds, curls, and tips of squash tendrils), finely chopped
½   teaspoon salt
       Freshly ground pepper

Makes 4 servings

In a medium skillet over medium heat, cook the onion in the olive oil, stirring often until softened, about 5 minutes. Stir in the tomatoes, cover, and cook over low heat until broken down, about 15 minutes.

Meanwhile, bring a large pot of lightly salted water to a boil. Add the *tenerumi* and cook until just tender, about 4 minutes. Drain in a fine sieve and let stand.

Stir the drained greens into the tomato mixture and cook for 2 to 3 minutes. Season with the salt and pepper. The *tenerumi* should be a thick mass. Serve at room temperature with a drizzle of olive oil.

MARGARET RUTA
Long Green Italian Squash

For years at Greenmarket I had seen a light green squash shaped like a long medieval trumpet, curled and twisted over on itself. I wasn't even sure it was edible, but Margaret Ruta, a customer, introduced me to this popular Mediterranean vegetable. Not only did she cook it in a traditional light tomato sauce, but to show me how good it was, she brought it back to me, warm from her kitchen. We ate it sitting together at the market.

This dish can be served over small macaroni such as orzo or orecchiette.

Makes 2 to 4 servings

3	tablespoons olive oil
1	medium onion, thinly sliced
1	medium ripe tomato, cut into small pieces
	Salt and freshly ground pepper
1	cup water, plus more if needed
1	long green Italian squash, peeled, seeded, cut into ¹/₂-inch thick slices, and halved lengthwise

Heat the oil in a large saucepan over medium-high heat and cook the onion, stirring, until opaque. Add the tomato, cook another 5 minutes, and season with salt and pepper. Add the water and cook 5 minutes longer. Add the squash, mixing well, and additional water if needed to cover. Cook until the squash is tender.

WALDY MALOUF

Roasted Trout with Summer Vegetables

Chef Waldy Malouf is a mentor for many of us at Greenmarket, supporting local farmers and helping us all to think seasonally. In this recipe, he combines the market's superb trout and prized summer vegetables.

The trout that we see in Greenmarket comes from the flowing spring-fed streams and ponds of Eden Brook Aquaculture in the Catskill Mountains, and its quality is unbelievable. It bears no resemblance to the more common farm-raised trout—fish that, in my opinion, is barely worth eating. If you've had a bad trout experience from store-bought fish or in a restaurant, forget it and go fishing at Greenmarket.

FOR THE SUMMER VEGETABLES

2	small Italian eggplant (about $1/4$ pound each), each cut in 6 diagonal slices
$1/3$	cup extra virgin olive oil
$1/2$	teaspoon salt
1	medium zucchini, cut on the bias into 12 slices
1	medium yellow summer squash, cut on the bias into 12 slices
$1/2$	cup shredded basil leaves
$1/8$	teaspoon freshly ground pepper
1	medium onion, halved and each half cut into 12 paper-thin slices
1	large ripe tomato, cut into 6 slices
	Basil leaves and lemon slices for garnish

Makes 4 servings

Preheat the broiler.

Arrange the eggplant slices on a lightly greased baking sheet. Brush with a little olive oil and sprinkle lightly with salt. Broil the eggplant 5 minutes on each side and let it cool. Turn the oven on to 450°F.

In a bowl, toss the zucchini and yellow squash with 3 tablespoons of the olive oil, the basil, ¼ teaspoon of the salt, and the pepper. On a greased baking sheet, stack the sliced vegetables in sets consisting of 1 slice each zucchini, yellow squash, onion, tomato, and eggplant, in 3 vertical rows. There will be 4 sets per row.

Roast the vegetables until tender, about 30 minutes. Using a spatula, lift sets of vegetables off the pan and arrange them decoratively around the edge of a large platter that will eventually hold the fish. The vegetables may be baked several hours in advance and served at room temperature.

FOR THE ROASTED TROUT

- 4 trout (12 ounces each), boned, heads removed and fins trimmed
  Salt
- 1/4 cup shredded basil leaves, plus leaves for garnish
- 1/4 cup fresh lemon juice
- 2 tablespoons extra virgin olive oil

Preheat the oven to 450°F.

Sprinkle the cavity of each trout lightly with salt (about 1 pinch per fish) and 1 tablespoon shredded basil. Oil a large roasting pan and lay the trout in it. Sprinkle the lemon juice and olive oil on top and roast until the fish is just cooked through, about 15 minutes.

Transfer the trout with a large spatula to the prepared platter. Pour the pan juices over the fish and garnish with the basil leaves.

Farmer Nicole Bishop and family

MICHAELA KANE SCHAEFFER
Scallops with Market Vegetable Sauce

Michaela Kane Schaeffer is a year-round Greenmarket regular who has offered us this summer dish, using fresh herbs and vegetables, including the little-known Lita squash. She tells us that it is delicious served over rice, pasta, polenta, or quinoa. It also can be made with diced, sautéed chicken breast or cooked lima or kidney beans, instead of the scallops.

If you come to the market very early—before seven in the morning—you will see women and young girls in traditional Middle Eastern dress, wearing black kerchiefs held on by colored bands, purchasing Lita squash. This small, light green, sweet vegetable is often passed over by the average market customer, but shoppers of Lebanese and Syrian ancestry know its value. It's a treasure that you might miss if you're not in the know, or if you are a late riser.

Makes 2 to 4 servings

2	tablespoons olive oil
1	onion, finely chopped
2	garlic cloves, minced
2	celery ribs, diced into 1/2-inch cubes
2	carrots, peeled and finely chopped
1	red bell pepper, finely diced
1/2	pound okra, sliced 1/2 inch thick
4	ripe tomatoes (or 8 plum tomatoes), coarsely chopped (seeded if desired)
1	to 2 Lita squash, sliced thin
1	teaspoon minced fresh thyme
2	to 3 basil leaves, finely chopped
1 1/2	teaspoons minced fresh rosemary leaves
1/2	cup dry white wine, or substitute broth or water
3	tablespoons fresh lemon juice
1	teaspoon Worcestershire sauce
1/2	teaspoon salt
1/4	teaspoon freshly ground pepper
1	pound sea scallops

Heat the oil in a large skillet over medium heat. Add the onion, garlic, celery, and carrot and cook, stirring occasionally, until tender, 5 to 7 minutes. Stir in the bell pepper, okra, tomatoes, squash, thyme, basil, rosemary, wine, lemon juice,

The Stark family of Eckerton Hill

Worcestershire sauce, salt, and pepper. Reduce the heat to low, cover, and simmer until the vegetables are tender and the flavors are blended, 10 to 12 minutes.

Add the scallops, cover, and simmer until they are no longer translucent, 3 to 4 minutes.

FIRST GARLIC
RAY BRADLEY

The earliest garlic to appear at market, "first garlic," although full-size, has not fully matured. A skin has not yet developed, and the "toes"—the unformed or undefined cloves—are not separated. All parts, except the stalk, are edible.

To cook, slice the garlic thinly and sauté in a little olive oil with some salt and pepper (add a bit of unsalted butter at the end).

Serve as a side dish or on top of chicken, meat, or fish.

ERICA DE MANE
Braised Chicken with Sweet Red Peppers and Fennel

Erica De Mane, a much-praised cookbook writer and one of our loyal customers, here takes simple chicken and spices it up in a nice markety way. It's a good dish for late summer, when bell peppers are ripe and fennel is sweet, and fresh tarragon is still available.

1	chicken, about 3½ pounds, cut into serving pieces
½ to ¾	teaspoon salt
	Freshly ground pepper
¼	cup flour for dredging the chicken
2	tablespoons olive oil
1	large onion, coarsely chopped
1	large fennel bulb (1¼ pounds), trimmed, quartered, cored, and thinly sliced, and some of the feathery top, coarsely chopped
2	small roasted red bell peppers (see page 15), cut into thin strips
½	cup dry white wine
½	cup chicken broth (or substitute 1 cup brown stock for the combined wine and broth)
1	tablespoon tarragon vinegar or white wine vinegar
2	tablespoons coarsely chopped fresh tarragon

Makes 3 to 4 servings

Season the chicken pieces with ¼ teaspoon each of salt and pepper, and coat with the flour, shaking off the excess.

Heat the olive oil until very hot in a large sauté pan over medium heat and sauté the chicken until browned, turning once, about 10 minutes. Remove the chicken to a plate. Pour off excess fat, if necessary. Add the onion and fennel and cook, stirring occasionally, until they begin to soften, about 6 minutes.

Add the red pepper strips and return the chicken to the pan. Pour in the wine and chicken broth and cover. Reduce the heat to low and simmer gently until the chicken is cooked through, about 30 minutes. Stir in the vinegar, a few fennel fronds, and the tarragon. Season with ¼ to ½ teaspoon salt (depending on the saltiness of the broth) and pepper to taste. Serve hot with rice or pasta.

TRACEY SEAMAN
Onion Lovers' Dip

Quark, sold by Hawthorne Valley Farm at the Union Square Greenmarket, is a tangy dairy product similar in texture and flavor to cream cheese but lower in fat and calories. Our recipe wizard, Tracy Seaman, serves this dip with potato chips and freshly cut-up market vegetables, and tells us it also makes a great baked potato topper. Feel free to add some chopped fresh herbs of your choice.

1/4	cup olive oil, preferably extra virgin
4	large shallots, peeled, halved, and thinly sliced
1	pound quark (or 8 ounces cream cheese at room temperature mixed with 8 ounces sour cream)
2	tablespoons fresh lime juice
1	teaspoon kosher salt
1/4	teaspoon freshly ground pepper
	Pinch of sugar
6	medium scallions, trimmed and thinly sliced
1	small red onion, peeled and finely diced
	Chips and assorted cut-up raw vegetables, for serving

Makes 3 cups

Heat the oil in a heavy skillet over mediuim-high heat until hot but not smoking. Add the shallots and cook, stirring often, until brown and crisp. Transfer to paper towels to drain and let cool.

In a large bowl, stir together the quark, lime juice, salt, pepper, and sugar until smooth. Stir in the scallions, red onion, and reserved shallots. Cover and refrigerate for 1 hour to let the flavors blend.

PEGGY KENT

Use-up-the-Fruit Pancake

Peggy Kent loves to cook, and fruit is her favorite food. She offered me this "great recipe" for using up leftover fruit—in her case, fruit that doesn't sell at the market or the Locust Grove Farms road stands. Made with any seasonal apples, berries, pears, grapes, plums, or cherries, it could carry you through summer and fall.

2	eggs
1	cup milk
2/3	cup all-purpose flour
2	tablespoons granulated sugar
1/2	teaspoon salt
1 1/2	tablespoons unsalted butter
5	to 6 cups whole berries or sliced seasonal fruit, pitted if necessary, such as apples, pears, peaches, grapes, plums, sweet cherries
1	to 4 tablespoons powdered sugar

Makes 4 to 6 servings

Preheat the oven to 400°F.

In a large bowl, whisk together the eggs, milk, flour, granulated sugar, and salt. (This can be done in a blender, if desired.)

Place the butter in a 9-inch cast-iron pan or round baking dish and melt in the oven. Pour the batter into the hot pan and spread evenly. Bake in the middle of the oven until puffy and deep brown, 30 to 35 minutes.

Meanwhile, in a large bowl, combine the fruit and powdered sugar to taste.

Sprinkle the pancake with powdered sugar to taste and top with the fruit salad. Cut into wedges and serve immediately.

RUTH REICHL
Apricot Pie

Ruth Reichl, the celebrated food writer and editor in chief of Gourmet *magazine, is a regular Greenmarket shopper. She says that this recipe works very well with mushy apricots, too ripe for easy eating, as well as with underripe apricots, which will require more sugar. (You can also use peaches; quarter them after pitting.) Serve some whipped cream or ice cream on top.*

1	stick (¹/₄ pound) unsalted butter
³/₄	cup light brown sugar (more if using underripe fruit)
³/₄	cup all-purpose flour
¹/₂	teaspoon grated nutmeg
2¹/₂	to 3 pounds apricots, peeled, halved, and pitted
1	prepared piecrust (see page 16)

Makes 8 servings

Preheat the oven to 450°F.

In a small saucepan over medium heat, melt the butter. Stir in the brown sugar. When melted, remove from the heat. Stir in the flour and nutmeg.

Pile the apricots into the prepared piecrust. Spread the butter mixture on top, patting it all the way to the edges.

Bake the pie in the bottom third of the oven for 10 minutes. Reduce the temperature to 350°F and bake 45 to 50 minutes longer, until the topping is golden brown and the apricots are very tender. Cover loosely with foil if the top is getting too brown. Let cool on a rack.

CONNIE McCABE
Mom's Cherry Pie

Connie McCabe, the talented food writer, fell in love with Greenmarket when she first came to New York City years ago. Connie's mom, Kate McCabe, had learned to make cherry pie from her own mother, Emma Traster, who had a huge garden, complete with cherry trees, in Hopkins, Misssouri. Kate now makes her famous pies using the cherries from her backyard tree in Kansas City. In New York, Connie uses Greenmarket cherries from Chip Kent and other farmers. Her crust isn't Mom's, but a variation of one taught her by the food expert John Willoughby.

Try this pie served with ice cream or whipped cream.

FOR THE PIECRUST
1½ cups all-purpose flour
½ teaspoon salt
½ cup cold vegetable shortening or lard
3 to 4 tablespoons ice water

Toss the flour and salt together in a large bowl and quickly cut in the cold shortening with two knives. When you have a bunch of small white pellets, drizzle the water into the mixture gradually, mixing with a fork until the dough is just wet enough to cling together. Shape the dough into a ball, wrap in wax paper, and refrigerate while you make the filling.

FOR THE FILLING
1⅓ cups sugar
⅓ cup all-purpose flour
⅛ teaspoon salt
5 to 6 cups pitted sour pie cherries
3 drops almond extract
2 tablespoons butter

Preheat the oven to 425°F.

Combine the sugar, flour, and salt in a small bowl. Place the cherries in a large bowl and add the almond extract. Toss well, then sprinkle the sugar and flour mixture over the cherries. Toss again.

To make the pie, divide the dough in half and shape into 2 disks. On a lightly floured surface, roll out one piece into an 11-inch circle. Fit the dough into a 9-

inch pie pan, spoon the cherries into the piecrust, and dot with the butter. Roll out the second disk; lay it on top of the cherries. Crimp the edges with your fingers or a fork. Cut 3 or 4 vents in the top and bake until steaming and golden, about 50 minutes. (If the edges of the crust start to brown, cover with foil.)

JIM FOBEL
Peach Coffee Cake

Jim Fobel—chef, cookbook author, and talented painter—has been shopping at Greenmarket since it first opened in 1976. Jim calls Ed and Carol Kesler of Tree-Licious Orchards the most wonderful farmers he has ever known, and adds: "They love to stop whatever they are doing to talk to their customers. Whether the conversation is about a recipe, heirloom gardening, their hens' laying habits, the weather, ice cream, or the traffic, they are always eager and enthusiastic." They have even offered to hold his many bags of produce and deliver them after the market has closed!

Jim makes this cake with their peaches every year.

Makes one 13 by 9-inch cake (12 to 16 servings)

FOR THE NUT TOPPING
- 1/4 cup all-purpose flour
- 1/4 cup packed light brown sugar
- 1/2 teaspoon ground cinnamon
- 2 tablespoons butter, softened
- 3/4 cup chopped walnuts or pecans

In a small bowl, combine the flour, brown sugar, and cinnamon. Rub in the butter to make the mixture crumbly, stir in the nuts, and reserve.

FOR THE CAKE
- 2 cups sifted cake flour (not self rising)
- 2 teaspoons baking powder
- 1/4 teaspoon salt
- 1 stick (8 tablespoons) butter, softened
- 1/4 cup vegetable shortening
- 3/4 cup sugar
- 3 large eggs, at room temperature
- 1 teaspoon grated lemon zest
- 2/3 cup milk, at room temperature
- 1 1/2 teaspoons vanilla extract
- 1/3 cup packed light brown sugar
- 1 teaspoon ground cinnamon
- 4 large peaches, peeled, halved, pitted, and cut into 1/2-inch slices (Use a vegetable peeler; or blanch the peaches for 15 seconds and then peel)

Preheat the oven to 350°F. Grease and flour a 13 by 9-inch cake pan.

In a medium bowl, stir together the cake flour, baking powder, and salt. Set aside.

In a large bowl, combine the butter, shortening, and sugar; beat with a hand-held electric mixer or wooden spoon until fluffy, 1 to 2 minutes. Beat in the eggs, one at a time, then the lemon zest. Beat in the flour mixture alternately with the milk and vanilla, about one quarter at a time, beginning and ending with the flour. The batter will be thick and fluffy.

In a small bowl, combine the brown sugar and cinnamon. Spread half the batter evenly into a thin layer in the prepared pan. Arrange all of the peach sices over the batter and sprinkle with the brown sugar mixture. Carefully spread the remaining batter evenly over the peaches. Crumble the reserved nut topping over the batter. Bake in the center of the oven for about 40 minutes, until a toothpick inserted near the center comes out clean and the edges of the cake barely begin to pull away from the sides of the pan.

Let cool completely in the pan on a rack. Cut into squares and serve warm or at room temperature, directly from the pan.

MELISSA CLARK

Golden Watermelon Ice

As a food writer, Melissa Clark has always tried to live within walking distance of a farmers' market. She describes her odyssey in search of "pristine produce": "First, I lived on the Upper West Side and would spend Sunday mornings browsing through the market on Seventy-seventh Street and Columbus Avenue. When I decamped downtown to Twenty-seventh Street and Lexington Avenue, I was but a few short blocks from the Union Square market, which has an amazing and inspirational variety of choices. Even near my next place in the East Village, there was a small weekend market on Avenue A where, in winter, I could find fresh cabbages and wrinkly heads of kale. Now, in Brooklyn, the Grand Army Plaza market is a pleasant stroll from my house. It was at this market that I first came across the succulent yellow-fleshed watermelons that got churned into this ice."

Melissa advises that red melons may be substituted for the yellow. Just get a sweet, juicy melon with no broken patches in the flesh. Serve the ice with whipped cream, if desired.

3   cups seeded, cubed yellow or red watermelon
(no larger than 1-inch cubes)

2   to 3 tablespoons Lyle's Golden Syrup
(available in large supermarkets)

Makes 4 servings

Place the watermelon in the freezer and let it freeze. It can be kept frozen for several weeks.

Before serving, place the melon cubes and the syrup in a food processor. Process until smooth, but don't overprocess and melt the mixture. Serve immediately.

WAYNE NISH

Cherry Soup with Black Mint and Lemon Sorbet

With his sunglasses and camera, Chef Wayne Nish of March restaurant has shopped at Greenmarket for many years unrecognized, and he has always been generous with his recipes. This easy-to-make soup is based on a variety of ripe, juicy cherries and mint, a perfect summer combination.

2 cups water
1 cup sugar
1/2 vanilla pod, beans scraped out
  Pinch salt
6 grinds black pepper
3 pounds mixed cherries (1 pound each dark sweet, sour, and Queen Anne), stemmed and pitted
1 bunch black mint (stems and leaves), bruised, plus extra for garnish
1 pint lemon sorbet, for serving

Makes 6 servings

In a small heavy saucepan, make a syrup by combining the water, sugar, vanilla pod, and salt and bring to a boil. Remove from the heat, add the pepper, and stir. Place the cherries and mint in a large bowl and pour the syrup on top. Let stand at room temperature until cool, then refrigerate until chilled, 2 to 3 hours or overnight. Remove the mint sprigs and vanilla pod.

To serve, place ½ cup of cherries with syrup in a bowl and top with a small scoop of lemon sorbet. Garnish with a sprig of mint.

TRACEY SEAMAN
Fresh Blackberry Ice Cream

In the summer, Tracey Seaman keeps her eyes peeled for the arrival of blackberries. Blackberry ice cream is one of her favorite berry sweets to make, because you can rarely buy it anywhere. She assures us that once you try a hot fudge sundae with this ice cream, your life will never be the same.

2¹/₂	cups heavy cream
1¹/₄	cups milk
1¹/₄	cups sugar (for very sweet berries, reduce the sugar to 1 cup)
1	vanilla pod, split lengthwise and beans scraped out
4	large egg yolks
2	pints fresh blackberries, picked through

Makes 1 quart

In a heavy medium saucepan over medium heat, combine the cream, milk, sugar, and vanilla pod. Stir often until the sugar dissolves and the mixture is steaming hot.

In a medium bowl, gently whisk the egg yolks. Carefully and slowly, gradually whisk in some of the hot cream mixture to heat the yolks. Scrape the mixture back into the saucepan, stirring to blend.

Cook over medium heat, whisking constantly, until the temperature of the mixture reaches 140°F on an instant-read thermometer, about 10 minutes. Remove from the heat, stir in the berries, and let stand until cool. Strain the custard through a fine sieve to remove the seeds; then cover and refrigerate until cold, about 2 hours or overnight.

Process the custard in an ice cream maker according to the manufacturer's instructions. For best results, serve at once.

Peach Jam

Although Stephanie was raised in France, she calls New York City home. Often in the summer I see her and her husband carrying away cases of produce from the market. This is her basic recipe for jam made from fresh market fruit. Make a batch in summer and it will last through the winter, reminding you of hot summer days.

7	pounds peaches, peeled, pitted, and coarsely chopped
3	pounds sugar (7 cups)
¼	cup lemon juice

Makes about 10 cups

Place the peaches in a 6-quart Dutch oven over medium heat, crushing them slightly with a potato masher, and cook until they start releasing juice, about 10 minutes. Stir in the sugar and lemon juice and reduce the heat to low. Cook, stirring and skimming any foam, until the jam is thickened slightly and translucent, about 1 hour.

Meanwhile, thoroughly wash 5 one-pint or 10 half-pint canning jars (such as Ball) in hot soapy water and rinse well. Place in a large Dutch oven filled with boiling water and boil for 20 minutes.

Ladle the hot jam into the hot jars, leaving ¼ inch head space. Cover the jars tightly with new lids. The jars can be stored in the refrigerator for up to 6 months.

Fall

Fall here in the Northeast is the time of harvest, when our market basket overflows and one basket is never enough for shopping. Lit by the autumn sun, the market is a festival of apples, grapes, tomatoes, and peppers; and as the weather cools, the fragile lettuce starts coming back. The herbs are lush and beautiful—it's time to buy bunches and dry them for winter. More and more of our customers appear, those who left the city for Memorial Day and returned after Labor Day, and our loyal summer regulars.

This is a celebratory time, with the expectation of Thanksgiving, the traditional harvest feast, in everyone's mind. You see real happiness on both sides of the tables. The farmers are reaping the rewards of their labors, with beautiful, high, long displays of ripe vegetables and fruits. They are continually asking the market managers if they can get just a little more display space, somehow get a few more feet, because the corn really is coming in, or the eggplants are overflowing, and they hadn't expected such high yields. The grape people hope to be selling their grapes right until Thanksgiving, maybe even later.

There is so much variety! Even assuming that I don't stop and visit every person I know, my market tour in the fall could take easily three hours, starting with the cut flowers and working all the way around to the squash. Things smell great and glisten—in a no-wax-added environment. As I walk around, I might get a glass of Ronnybrook milk, or an Asian pear from the Lees, and I'll stop at Ann Salomon's stand and have some soothing herbal tea. Fall is the time to soak in the beauty of the mounds of root crops, coppery carrots, and earth-toned beets. They are piled so high that they catch your eye from blocks away. I always see someone trying to carry out an enormous banana squash—sometimes over four feet long. When I walk through the market, drinking in all the colors and inhaling the aromas of the farm, orchard, and vineyard, I have to smile. I love being part of it.

Filling Your Market Basket in Fall
October, November, December

Cut Flowers and Vines
Eucalyptus
Flowering Kale
Salvia
Ornamental Pepper
Bittersweet
Rosehip

Ornamental Garden Starters
Rosemary
Mum
Lily
Aster
Poinsettia
Scented Geranium

Freshly Cut Herbs
Flowering Dill

Chive Blossoms
Basil: Genovese; Napoletano; Anise (Thai or Licorice); Purple (Opal)
Anise Hyssop
Oregano
Rosemary
Sage
Thyme
Marjoram
Chervil
Parsley
English Black Peppermint
Egyptian Peppermint

Edible Flowers
Sage: Honey Melon; Pineapple

Cilantro Flower
Dianthus (Carnation; Pink)
Nasturtium
Zucchini Blossom
Rosemary Flowers

Lettuce
Batavian or French (Canasta)
Butterhead or Bibb (Brune d'Hiver)
Crisphead or Iceberg (Chou de Naples)
Cos or Romaine (Little Gem)
Looseleaf (Black-Seeded Simpson)

Salad and Cooking Greens
Mâche
Arugula
Dandelion, Red or Green
Bronze Fennel
Red Mustard
Radicchio
Red Orach (Mountain Spinach)
Wild Watercress
Pepper Cress
Upland Cress
Baby Kale (Red Russian or Blue Siberian)
Collards
Broccoli Rabe (Rapini)
Choy Sum
Mibuna

Spinach
Amaranth
Swiss Chard

Vegetables
Beans, Shelling: Fava
(Broad Bean); Soy
(Edamame); Lima
Beans, Snap: String, Pole,
Bush
French Filet (Haricot
Vert)
Summer Squash: Scallop;
Zucchini; Cocozelle
(Marrow); Lita
(Lebanese); Ronde de
Nice; Yellow Crook-
neck; Cucuzzi (Bottle
Gourd; Long Green);
Tenerumi (Squash Run-
ners)
Corn: Bi-color; White;
Yellow
Broccoli
Cabbage (Red and
Green)
Savoy Cabbage
Cauliflower: White; Broc-
coflower (Cauli-Broc);
Romanesco Broccoli;
Purple
Brussels Sprouts
Cucumber: Jersey Pickle;
Lemon; Aria; Suyo
Long
Fennel
Celery; Red Celery
Bitter Melon
Eggplant: Bambino; Rosa
Bianca; Kermit (Thai);

Turkish Orange
Peppers: Bell; Frying;
Hot; Spice
Pumpkin
Winter Squash

Dried Beans
Cranberry
Great Northern
Jacob's Cattle
Navy
Pinto
Red Kidney
Black Turtle

Cultivated Mushrooms
Button
Cremini
Portobello
Shiitake

Wild Mushrooms
Oyster (Tree Mushroom,
Hiratake)
Horse Mushroom (Field)
Porcini (Cèpe)
Hen of the Woods

Root Crops
Beet: Red; White; Golden;
Striped (Chioggia or
Candy Cane)
Leek
Scallion
Carrot: Baby; Orange;
Yellow; Belgian White;
Red
Jerusalem Artichoke
(Sunchoke)
Onion: Red Torpedo;

White Bermuda; Walla
Walla; Sweet Flat Red;
Cippolini; Ailsa Craig
Garlic (Rocambole or Top
Setting Varieties)
Shallot
Parsley Root
Celeriac
Sweet Potato
Rutabaga
Turnip
Daikon
Black Radish
Horseradish
Parsnip

Fruit
Raspberry: Red; Purple;
Black; Yellow
Strawberry
Grapes, Seedless:
Canadice; Einset; Him-
rod; Vanessa
Grapes, Seeded: Caco;
Catawba; Concord; Di-
amond; Niagara
Pears, Asian: Kosui (Good
Water); Seuri; Shin-
seiki (New Century)
Pears, Western: Clapp's
Favorite (Red Clapp's
Favorite); Bartlett;
Bosc; Devoe; Seckle
Quince
Cranberry

Nuts
Black Walnut
Butternut (White Walnut)

Poultry, Meat, and Game
Venison
Muscovy Duck
Pekin Duck
Pheasant
Partridge
Wild Turkey
Domestic Turkey
Goose
Guinea Hen
Capon
Quail
Wild Boar
Chicken

Fish and Seafood
Fluke (Summer Flounder)
Blackfish
Butterfish
Skate
Striped Bass
Monkfish
Lobster
Smoked Fish

Also available in fall
dried grains, dried flow-
ers and grasses; honey;
maple syrup; prepared
products such as
eggnog, jams, cider,
and candy apples; and
seasonal baked goods,
such as pumpkin pie,
squash pie, cakes, and
muffins.

Fall

ORGANIC
MESCLUN
WASHED READY TO EAT
SALAD MIX

Sage
$1.00 per bunch

23 DEWOLF ROAD
OLD TAPPAN N.J.

Leeks

BRUSSEL
SPROUT
2.00/STALK
2 FOR

MIGLIORELLI FARM
TIVOLI, N.Y.

BLUE
FRESH FISH

Quince

Fall Recipes

MARKET PEOPLE
Stephanie Villani

Stephanie and her husband, Alex, of Saltwater Enterprises in Mattituck, New York, can be found at their Blue Moon fish and seafood stand at the Union Square Greenmarket. Stephanie describes the market mystique:

"After working at the market for so many years, I still see the longing and the envy a lot of people have for our lifestyle. Many customers would love to be outside working on a boat or a farm. It's a very romantic notion. Of course, they don't realize the long hard work that goes into the markets. We are here every week, no exceptions, in good weather and bad. People always ask, 'What time do you get up in the morning?' (3:15 A.M.!) 'What time do you leave your house?' 'How long does it take you to get here?'"

"When I lived in Manhattan, I used to hate shopping at grocery stores—many of the checkout people didn't acknowledge you, and half the time they didn't know what they were doing. At the market, the sellers are the producers and they can tell you almost anything you want to know—maybe more than you want to know—about what they are selling.

"We carry home unbelievable produce throughout the year and I hardly ever go to the grocery store if I can help it. I get cheese, milk, all kinds of bread, sausage, turkey, meat, eggs. The array of produce is really astonishing.

"Tim Stark has incredible peppers and heirloom tomatoes. Our neighbors have these beautiful radishes and carrots—they look so good they almost look fake. I learned to use herbs I'd never heard of, like anise hyssop and chervil, as well as lavender, lemon thyme, and lots of others."

Stephanie Villani

MARKET PEOPLE
Chip Kent

I first met Chip Kent when I was the manager of a small Greenmarket in a schoolyard on the corner of Amsterdam Avenue and West 102nd Street in Manhattan. It was a scorching summer day; the heat rising up from the blacktop was enough to make baked Alaska, with a side order of eggs over easy. As I melted at the manager's table, I spied Chip filling plastic bags with water from a fire hydrant. He carried them back to his

Chip Kent

started to laugh. After she gave her son a proper inspection, all was forgiven. "Chip," she asked, "Will you ever grow up?" She left, waving good-bye, and called out: "See you next week, and try to stay out of trouble!"

Now, years later, Chip is still throwing water balloons. He married his best friend, Peggy, and their three young children may well be the third generation of Kents to sell apples at Greenmarket.

Apples

There are apples, and then there are apples. Everyone has eaten Red Delicious and McIntosh, but how many of us would recognize Black Twig, Eve's Delight, or Northern Spy? If the only place you shop for fruit is your supermarket (even if it professes to have a "farmers' market" for produce), chances are you will have fewer than six varieties of apples to choose from. McIntosh, Red and Golden Delicious, and, most assuredly, Granny Smith from New Zealand will make up more than half the display.

These apples are available throughout the year; they no longer have a season. Their place of origin may be Chile or South Africa, or perhaps a huge corporate farm in Washington state, and each will wear an individual sticker. Red or green, each will be cosmetically good, with well-rounded shoulders and four perfect points on the bottom, and will shine like a West Point cadet's dress shoes or a new Buick on the showroom floor. Your assembly-line apples certainly won't make you think of fragrant orchards of gnarled fruit trees with dandelions dancing around their roots.

It is true that these apples ship well and can stay firm for a long time on the grocer's shelf. But the larger truth is that they have no distinct taste and the

stall and began to hurl them at co-workers and neighboring farmers. With a shiny new manager's button pinned to my T-shirt and too noble a sense of order in my dehydrated brain, I ran over and ordered him to stop before somebody got hurt. Chip flashed his winning smile and as the words "Sure, Joel," left his mouth, he hurled the last two bags straight at me. One hit me full in the chest. The second, stalled in flight by the thick air of the hot day, seemed to float toward me. I reached out for it, but it picked up momentum, escaping my grasp, and as I watched in horror, it landed on a toddler seated in his stroller. A lot passed through my mind in the absolute silence that followed, while I waited for the child's tears and his mother's screams.

Greenmarket, fortunately, brings out the best in people. The little guy, unhurt, began to giggle. As far as he was concerned, being hit by a cold-water balloon on a hot summer's day was great fun. In turn, his mom

Chip Kent

APPLE TIPS

Buying Skin with a waxy bloom (whitish film), bumps, or russeting (rough texture) in no way affects the apple's flavor or quality. A good apple doesn't need to win a beauty contest. • Hold the fruit in your hand. It should have no visible bruises, and should be firm to the touch. *Storing* Refrigerate apples, but remove from the fridge 15 minutes or so before consumption. They should be eaten close to room temperature.

uniform consistency of wet cardboard. And all this uniformity and perfection leave no room for Golden Russet, Wolf River, or any of the more than three hundred varieties of apples grown in the United States.

Leave your supermarket behind and find the real farmers' market in your area. Become acquainted with an orchardist and let him or her guide you through your region's apple season—the first thing you will learn is not to reject ugly apples.

Greenmarket apples won't be waxed, because they are meant to be eaten today or tomorrow, not to

be kept for months in a bowl in your den. They may be uneven in shape, or have bumps or rough patches of skin, but beauty is only skin deep!

Apple Chart

The Kents' Locust Grove Farms was established in 1820 in Milton, New York. Today, Chip Kent and his wife, Peggy—along with Chip's parents, brother, sister, aunt Kathleen, uncle Oliver, and the rest of the extended family—live there and grow apples, pears, cherries, and vegetables. The first word that Chip's son Aaron spoke was *apple,* which happened to indicate his first solid food.

With Chip and other members of the Kent family, I have developed this all-purpose guide to using his "Locally Groan" fruit. (Chip is as famous for his offbeat sense of humor as he is for his encyclopedic knowledge of apples.)

Chip's Uncle Oliver

Chip's Favorite Apples

Variety and History	Appearance and Taste	Let's Eat!
Akane (pronounced ah-cahn-nuh) A cross between Jonathan and Worcester Pearmain, developed in Japan in the 1970s.	More flat than round, this bright red apple looks like someone sat on it. Juicy, aromatic, toothsome.	A perfect choice to mix in applesauce. Leave a few slices with their peels intact to give your sauce added aroma and a pinkish hue.
Baldwin Culinary historian and author Anne Mendelson reports that the *Baldwin* originally was called "Woodpecker." It was the number one apple consumed by New Yorkers prior to the arrival of the *McIntosh* and *Red Delicious*.	"The Ford Model T of apples," Chip calls it—classically tart and full-flavored.	*Baldwin*'s spiciness makes it a welcome addition in fresh cider, pies, and sauces. Great for munching.
Black Twig Good luck trying to find a *Black Twig* at your local supermarket! Farmers' markets are the best source.	Chip's "Guinness Stout of apples." Dark-red—almost purple—with hard, juicy, fragrant, golden flesh and grassy, intense flavor. "Take a bite and it will bite you back," he says.	Excellent for eating out of hand.
Chipper Unique to Locust Grove. When Chip was 14, a chance seedling came up in the plum orchard. To protect the tree and prove to his family that the fruit was edible, he ate it all.	A good-looking apple with an intense personality and a sobering, mildly acidic taste. Harvested around October 1, Chip's birthday. He says it is "very popular."	Eat out of hand; good for sauce.
Cortland A larger version of the *McIntosh*. Cross between *McIntosh* and *Ben Davis*.	Chip calls it the "Bite Me—Bake Me—Eat Me" apple. Has a shiny red skin with subtle striping. A mild tasting apple with a good balance of tart and tang.	Good for eating out of hand and wonderful in salads and other uncooked dishes because its flesh is slow to oxidize (turn brown). Also good for sauces and pies.
Cox's Orange Pippin One of England's most popular apples. Seldom available in the U.S. outside of farmers' markets, because local weather may cause low yields.	Crisp and juicy with excellent flavor. Skin is clear yellow, with orange and red stripes.	Perfect for eating out of hand. Fine for appplesauce or blended with other varieties in a pie.

Fall

Variety and History	Appearance and Taste	Let's Eat!
Empire A cross between *Red Delicious* and *McIntosh,* developed in the 1960s by the Geneva, New York, Agricultural Experiment Station.	"Bite me—Eat me—Bake me" Red, with a natural bloom (off-white, dusty overtone), speckled skin, and creamy white flesh. Crackling, tangy, with a nice snap when bitten into.	Good in salads or eaten out of hand.
Eve's Delight Large, up to 2 pounds. One apple is big enough to make a pie.	Red with yellow undertones. Big, tangy flavor.	Good for eating out of hand (if you're strong and hungry) and in pies.
Fuji Cross between the older *Ralls Janet* and the *Red Delicious,* esteemed in Japan and China. First popular on the West Coast, now grown by East Coast farmers.	Golden-brown skin with a distinctive red blush and unforgettable honeylike taste. Sweet and juicy.	Use in applesauce blends, eat it out of hand, or slice onto buttered toast. Too hard for pies.
Gala When selecting fruit, size doesn't always matter.	On the small side, with glossy, bright yellow skin, covered with orange-red stripes. Crunchy texture combined with a sweetish, tangy, light taste.	Not for cooking, but a perfect choice when packing your children's lunch or your own.
Golden Delicious Not related to *Red Delicious*. The second-most-consumed apple in the world after "Big Red." When grown in New York, often gets a skin blemish, called russeting, a rough, brownish spot that has no effect on taste. Does not keep well at room temperature.	Best eaten when the skin is pale yellow with an occasional pink blush—"a kiss from the sun," Chip calls it. Tangy, juicy, with a mild but sweet taste.	Fine for eating out of hand. Holds its shape well for pies, tarts, and other cooked desserts.
Golden Russet An old variety, hard to find outside of farmers' markets. Keeps well in storage.	Light reddish-green skin with occasional yellow-golden blemishes that don't affect flavor—to Chip, "part of the apple's natural charm." Tart and hard.	Good for use in hard and fresh cider and eating out of hand.

Variety and History	Appearance and Taste	Let's Eat!
Jonagold Cross between *Jonathan* and *Golden Delicious*. Developed by the Geneva, New York, Agricultural Experiment Station. Growing popularity in New York and other East Coast markets.	Crimson skin with greenish-yellow undertones and a plump, round shape. Sweet-tart, very crunchy, juicy white flesh.	Best eaten out of hand; makes a nice addition to applesauce.
Jonathan An elder statesperson of apples that reminds us that older is often better. This locally developed variety first appeared in the Hudson Valley region during the early 1800s and still remains a grower and consumer favorite.	Round, red-skinned apple with yellow undertones. Tangy, crackly, spicy. Crisp, finely textured, juicy flesh.	A perfect choice for eating out of hand or fresh juicing. Excellent for all cooking purposes.
McIntosh Developed by John McIntosh on his farm in Canada around 1870, from parent apples *Fameuse* and *Red Detroit*. One of the most popular apples in the northeastern United States.	Red skin with white tender flesh. "Crisp, tangy, drippy, spicy, and aromatic," Chip says.	Excellent for sauce; very good for juicing or cider. Not the best choice for pies, will not hold their shape.
Macoun (pronounced ma-cow-in) A popular apple, born around 1923.	Somewhat squat shape; dull red skin, coated with a natural film often mistaken for added wax. Crackly, semitart, very crisp and tangy.	Best eaten out of hand and baked in pies.
Mutsu A popular apple developed in Japan; renamed *Crispin* when it traveled to Europe and America.	At first glance this large, round apple is often mistaken for a *Golden Delicious,* but it is harder. Pale yellow, with an occasional light-red blush when ripe. Crunchy, tangy.	Best eaten out of hand. Excellent in pies.

Variety and History	Appearance and Taste	Let's Eat!
Newtown Pippin This hard-to-find apple is a true New Yorker, grown before the American Revolution in what is now the Borough of Queens. A favorite of George Washington, Thomas Jefferson, and Benjamin Franklin.	Skin is a mixture of pale green and soft yellow, with an occasional red streak. *Pippins* have a faint citrus scent and a complex, balanced, sweet-and-tart taste.	Excellent eaten out of hand, and just as good in applesauce or pies.
Northern Spy An old-school New York State classic. The skin bruises easily, which is why you rarely find it outside farmers' markets.	Chip calls this "the master apple"—as in master spy. Large, round shape with pale yellow, pink-to-red-blushed skin. Crisp, very juicy, richly flavored, aromatic.	Always at home in pies or sauce; good eaten out of hand.
Opalescent Often waxy to the touch in their natural state so don't get nervous that the farmer has added an extra coating.	"Crunchable, munchable," Chip says. Large, round, with big shoulders. Skin has a bright, pale-yellow layer covered in dark red. Mild, sweet flavor and dry, nutty texture.	Excellent eaten out of hand and in pies. Breaks into chunks when cooked.
Red Delicious Hard to find a decent one outside a farmers' market. Their mass marketing has been so successful that it is not uncommon to see them months after their harvest time has passed.	Shaped like a long tooth with deep-red color, skin that is often chewy and bitter, and yellow flesh. "Sweet, tight, and drippy," as Chip describes it; slightly tart and aromatic.	Best eaten out of hand but be warned—it will keep its good looks long after its taste and texture are gone.
Rhode Island Greening At the turn of the century, *Baldwins* were the only tart apples more popular than Greenings.	Sour and hard with distinctive tart flavor and soft grassy-colored skin. When it comes to tart, spicy apples, this beats the *Granny Smith* any day.	Very good for eating out of hand and excellent for pies.
Rome Named for Rome Township, Ohio. Don't confuse it with the more modern *Rome Beauty*—this classic is much better.	Large, round, yellow- to green-skinned fruit with mottled red overtones, crunchy texture, and tangy flavor. Becomes mealy and flavorless when stored too long.	At its best as a baked apple.

Variety and History	Appearance and Taste	Let's Eat!
Stayman A popular offspring of the *Winesap*.	Rich red color with green undertones. Firm flesh and complex flavor.	A good all-purpose apple.
Sweet Sixteen Available at farmers' markets. Popular with those in the know.	A medium- to large-size apple with striped red skin and creamy-colored flesh. Juicy and aromatic with hints of anise.	Excellent for eating out of hand.
Tydeman's Early Red One of the best early season apples, harvested in the New York area in late August or early September.	Thin skin with a naturally waxy feeling. Not quite round. Somewhat perfumed.	Best eaten out of hand while we wait for its more tasty cousins to ripen.
Twenty Ounce Introduced in the 1840s in Connecticut and New York. Its weight often equals its name.	Very large; skin is yellow-green splashed with bright red. Tart flavor.	Best used for cooking, but eat it out of hand to enjoy subtle characteristics.
Winesap Popularity is high among Greenmarket shoppers.	On the small side with winy flavor and juicy, firm flesh. Hard and tangy.	Eat it as is or try it in your favorite apple recipe.
Winter Banana Thought to have originated in the Midwest from a random seedling.	Truly a beautiful apple to behold, its waxy, lemon-yellow skin is highlighted with a rosy blush. Mild-flavored, crisp, and juicy.	Not up to our standards for cooking but fine for everyday eating.
Wolf River Originated in the late 1800s in Wisconsin. Popular in the Midwest.	Large and somewhat irregularly shaped—more flat than round. Bright-yellow skin is blushed over with rich, bright red. Tart flavor.	Nice for eating out of hand or try it in apple butter. Good for pies and drying.
York Imperial Originated in York County, Pennsylvania, in the 1800s.	Off-center, lopsided shape; yellow- and pink- to red-blushed skin, with fire engine–red streaks. Juicy and mildly sweet.	A good choice for drying. Its color lends a nice tint to pies and sauces.

KENNETH JOHNSON
Chilled Parsnip and Apple Soup

Kenneth Johnson, a New York City chef, is popular for his winning food. The unusual combination of apples and parsnips really works in this soup, and a garnish of crisp fried parsnip slices brings the dish together.

Makes 6 servings

FOR THE APPLE CONFIT

2	cups apple cider
1	sprig tarragon
2	Mutsu or Golden Delicious apples, peeled, cored, and cut into 1/4-inch dice

Bring the cider to a boil in a medium saucepan, add the tarragon and the apples, and poach the apples until tender, about 10 minutes. Drain and refrigerate in a bowl, until ready to use (up to 2 days ahead; the liquid may be saved for another use).

FOR THE SOUP

2	tablespoons unsalted butter
1	medium onion, coarsely chopped
1/2	celery stalk, sliced
2	medium Mutsu apples, peeled and coarsely chopped
1 1/2	pounds parsnips, peeled and coarsely chopped
2	tablespoons white wine
1 1/2	tablespoons Calvados
1/2	cup whole milk
2	cups water
1/2	teaspoon cardamom seeds
	Kosher salt and freshly ground pepper

In a large saucepan over medium heat, melt the butter and cook the onions and celery, stirring occasionally, until soft, 8 to 10 minutes. Add the apples and parsnips and cook an additional 5 minutes. Add the wine and Calvados, bring to a boil, and boil 2 minutes. Add the milk, water, and cardamom. Simmer the mixture until tender, about 1 hour. Puree in a blender. Season with salt and pepper to taste and refrigerate.

Vegetable oil for frying

2   small parsnips, peeled and cut into long strips with a potato peeler

Kosher salt and freshly ground pepper

Chopped tarragon, for garnish

In a large saucepan over medium-high heat, heat the oil to 325°F, or until a piece of parsnip sizzles when immersed. Fry the parsnip strips in batches until golden brown. Drain on paper towels and season with salt and pepper to taste while still warm.

TO SERVE

Ladle the soup into chilled bowls. Garnish each with a tablespoon of apple confit and top with crisp parsnips. Sprinkle with chopped tarragon.

Jan Czech of Terhune Orchards

LESLIE McKEN

Chile Pumpkin Soup

Leslie McKen is the chef at Brooklyn's New Prospect at Home food shop, where local ciders and cheeses, as well as apples still in their crates and straight from Greenmarket, are for sale. This pumpkin soup is spiced with chiles and served with a roasted corn relish, making good use of end-of-season corn. Its fall colors are striking, with the deep rust of the soup set off by the dark-red puree, yellow corn, and sour cream. Cheese pumpkins are named for the old-fashioned cheese boxes they resemble.

FOR THE ROASTED CORN RELISH

2	cups fresh corn kernels
1	teaspoon olive oil
1	clove garlic, minced
	Salt and freshly ground pepper
3	tablespoons chopped cilantro
1/4	teaspoon grated lemon zest
1	teaspoon lemon juice

Makes 3 quarts

Preheat the oven to 350°F.

In a small bowl, toss together the corn, olive oil, garlic, salt, and pepper. Place in a baking dish and roast 20 minutes. Mix in the cilantro, lemon zest, and lemon juice and season with salt and pepper.

FOR THE CHILE PUREE

2	dried ancho chiles, stemmed and seeded
1	roasted red bell pepper (see page 15)
1	teaspoon sherry vinegar
1	teaspoon honey
1/4	teaspoon salt
	Freshly ground pepper to taste

In a small pot, cover the chiles with boiling water and simmer until soft. Place in a food processor or blender with 1 roasted bell pepper, sherry vinegar, honey, salt, and pepper and process until pureed. Strain and reserve.

FOR THE PUMPKIN SOUP

1   dried ancho chile, seeded and broken
2   tablespoons olive oil
1   cheese pumpkin (3 pounds), peeled, seeded, and cubed
3   onions, coarsely chopped (2 cups)
4   cloves garlic, peeled and smashed
1   tablespoon fresh thyme
1   tablespoon chile powder
2   bay leaves
2   cups chopped tomatoes, fresh or canned, finely diced
2   roasted red bell peppers, coarsely chopped (see page 15)
8   cups chicken or vegetable stock (or 4 cups stock and 4 cups water)
1   tablespoon honey
1   cup cream, optional
1   teaspoon salt
    Freshly ground pepper to taste
    Sour cream or crème fraîche, chile puree, and corn relish, for garnish

In a small pot, cover the chile with boiling water and simmer until soft.

In a large pot over medium heat, heat the oil. Add the pumpkin, onions, and garlic and cook, stirring often, until softened, about 15 minutes. Add the chile, thyme, chile powder, bay leaves, tomatoes, and bell peppers. Pour in the stock and bring to a boil, reduce the heat, and simmer for 1 hour.

Remove the bay leaves. Puree the soup in a blender in batches, a few cups at a time. Return the soup to the pot; stir in the honey and cream, and season with salt and pepper.

Ladle into bowls, drizzle some chile puree onto the soup, and run a knife or spoon through the puree to make an attractive pattern, if desired. Top with a dollop of sour cream or crème fraîche, and sprinkle with the roasted corn relish.

JULIE AND DAVID YEN

Stuffed Bitter Melon with White Soup

With its waxy, bumpy, pale- to dark-green skin, bitter melon is not often praised for its looks. As the name indicates, it has a somewhat bitter flavor, to which water chestnuts, ground fish or meat, and hot pepper add pleasant contrast. The Yens have introduced this Asian gourd (it's not a melon in the musk or watermelon style) to Greenmarket.

1/2	pound ground fish, pork, chicken, or beef
3	large water chestnuts, finely chopped
3	scallions; 2 minced, 1 thinly sliced for garnish
1	large carrot, sliced into slivers
1	tablespoon cornstarch
3	tablespoons olive oil
1/8	teaspoon sea salt
1/8	teaspoon freshly ground black pepper
1 1/2	pounds bitter melon, cut into 8 slices and seeded
5	cups vegetable or chicken broth (see pages 14-15)
2	hot peppers, seeded and thinly sliced

Makes 4 servings

In a large bowl, mix together the fish or meat, chopped water chestnuts, minced scallions, carrot, cornstarch, 1 tablespoon oil, salt, and pepper, using your hands.

Place the bitter melon slices on a work surface. Fill the center of each slice with the stuffing mixture, taking care not to overfill.

Heat the remaining olive oil in a large skillet over medium heat. Add the bitter melon slices and cook, turning occasionally, until both sides are golden brown and the filling is firm, 8 to 10 minutes.

Meanwhile, in a saucepan over medium heat, bring the broth to a simmer. Add the cooked melon slices, cover, and simmer gently for 10 minutes.

Divide the soup and melon among 4 bowls. Garnish with the remaining scallion and the hot pepper.

JULIE AND DAVID YEN
Bitter Melon Salad

Recently, bitter melons have become part of the colorful display at the farm stands of the Yen family and other Greenmarket growers. Their bizarre, alligator-like skin makes shoppers stop and stare, but seldom do they purchase them. Perhaps this recipe will serve as encouragement.

Serve as a side dish with fish, poultry, or vegetables.

2	bitter melons (about $1/2$ pound each), halved lengthwise, seeded, and sliced paper thin
1	tablespoon sea salt or kosher salt
1	scallion, minced
2	large garlic cloves, peeled
1	teaspoon sugar, optional
$1/4$	cup sesame oil
	Rice wine vinegar
2	large shiso or basil leaves, finely chopped (1 tablespoon)

Makes 6 servings

In a large colander, mix the melon slices and the sea salt. Mix until all the slices are well coated with salt. Let stand 15 minutes.

Rinse the melon with hot tap water. Drain and rinse at least twice more, until all the salt has been removed. When the salt is gone, rinse the bitter melon in cold water and drain.

In a large bowl, combine the melon, with the remaining ingredients. Mix well with your hands, almost in a kneading motion.

Push the mixture snugly into the bottom of the bowl. Cover the bowl with plastic wrap and chill for 10 minutes before serving.

PETER IVY

Roasted Beet, Pear, and Leek Salad with Gorgonzola Croutons

This salad from Chef Peter Ivy uses ingredients basic to the fall market basket. If you want to be a little brave, why not try it with New York's Berkshire Blue Goat Cheese from Little Rainbow Chèvre?

4	small beets, trimmed and scrubbed
3/4	cup walnuts
3	tablespoons balsamic vinegar
1/3	cup olive oil
1	tablespoon coarse-grain mustard
1	teaspoon finely chopped fresh rosemary
1	tablespoon honey
	Salt and freshly ground pepper
3	pears, such as Bartlett or Bosc, cored and cut into 8 wedges each
8	baby leeks (or 12 scallions), green portions and roots removed, washed well
1	cup crumbled Gorgonzola cheese
2	tablespoons olive oil
1	small baguette, sliced crosswise into sixteen 1/2-inch croutons

Makes 4 servings

Preheat the oven to 400°F.

Place the beets in a single layer on a 12-inch square of foil. Wrap into a package and roast in the oven for 45 minutes. Let cool, then gently rub off their skins with a paper towel and cut each into 6 wedges. Set aside.

Meanwhile, place the walnuts on a large baking sheet. Toast in the oven about 10 minutes. Let cool, then coarsely chop half of the nuts. Set aside.

To make the vinaigrette, whisk together the balsamic vinegar, olive oil, mustard, rosemary, and honey in a small bowl. Season with salt and pepper to taste. Reserve 1/2 cup. Separately toss the roasted beet wedges, raw pears, and leeks with 3 tablespoons of dressing each. Arrange in a single layer on a large baking pan and cook in the hot oven until soft, about 20 minutes for the pears and 10 minutes for the leeks (or scallions). Let cool to room temperature. The vegetables and pears can be roasted 1 day ahead, cooled, wrapped separately, and refrigerated. Let stand at room temperature 1 to 2 hours before serving.

In a small bowl, stir the Gorgonzola cheese, olive oil, and half of the walnuts to make a paste. Spread on the croutons and bake until the topping melts, about 10 minutes.

Arrange the roasted fruit and vegetables on 4 dinner plates and sprinkle with the reserved nuts. Garnish each plate with 4 croutons.

Ging Lee of Pittstown Fruit Farm with friend

DAVID PAGE

Apple Slaw with Horseradish Dressing

This tempting recipe from Chef David Page makes use of Greenmarket's fall harvest. You can make this tasty slaw quickly in a food processor—mix the dressing first, then shred and grate the ingredients for the slaw. Feel free to use red or green cabbage, or a combination of the two.

FOR THE DRESSING

- 2 cloves garlic
- 1/4 cup olive oil
- 3 tablespoons grated fresh horseradish
- 1 small shallot, peeled and halved
- 2 tablespoons tarragon vinegar, or white wine vinegar
- 2 teaspoons Dijon mustard
- 2 tablespoons honey
- 2 tablespoons water
- 1/4 teaspoon salt
- 1/4 teaspoon freshly ground pepper

Makes 6 to 8 servings

Preheat the oven to 400°F.

Place the garlic cloves on a 12-inch square of foil and drizzle with 1/2 tablespoon of the oil. Fold up the ends of the foil to seal. Bake for 40 minutes. Let cool and then unwrap the garlic. Peel the cloves and mash. You should have about 2 tablespoons.

In a food processor combine the garlic, horseradish, shallot, vinegar, mustard, and honey. With the motor running, slowly add the oil until emulsified. Adjust the consistency with water, and season with salt and pepper.

FOR THE SLAW

- 3 cups shredded red cabbage (1/4 medium head)
- 3 cups shredded green cabbage (1/4 medium head)
- 1 Mutsu apple, cored and coarsely grated
- 1 large carrot, peeled and coarsely grated
- 1/3 cup packed chopped flat-leaf parsley
- 1 tablespoon whole mustard seed, toasted in a skillet over medium heat until it pops

In a large bowl, combine the slaw ingredients. Add the horseradish dressing and mix well.

KATHERINE ALFORD
Oven-Dried Tomatoes

Food writer and instructor Katherine Alford has put together this simple recipe that will help you use fall's ripe plum tomatoes and fresh herbs. Slow-cooking the tomatoes in the oven brings out their best qualities.

2	pounds ripe plum tomatoes, cored and cut in half lengthwise
1	teaspoon kosher salt
2	cups extra virgin olive oil
2	large fresh thyme sprigs
1	fresh rosemary sprig, cut in half
2	to 3 fresh sage leaves
3	medium garlic cloves, cut in half

Makes 6 to 8 servings

Place the tomatoes on a baking sheet and sprinkle with the salt. Let rest for 30 minutes. Preheat the oven to 250°F.

Pat the tomatoes dry and put them in the oven. Let them oven dry for 5 to 6 hours, until they are dried but still slightly plump. They should not be leathery.

Place the tomatoes in a jar or bowl with the olive oil, herbs, and garlic. Cover and refrigerate overnight or up to 2 weeks.

Tony Mannetta,
Greenmarket director

MICHAEL KRONDL

Zucchini and Roasted Pepper Tians with Golden Tomato Coulis

Michael Krondl is a market customer, a food historian, and a cooking instructor at the New School. We've taught a class together, where I guided the market half and he led the cooking half. When we talked about recipes, he offered this one, which highlights the robust tastes of fall vegetables along with the last of the summer herbs and tomatoes.

FOR THE ZUCCHINI AND ROASTED PEPPER TIANS

Makes 6 servings

3	tablespoons olive oil
1	small onion, finely chopped
2	medium zucchini, finely diced
3	medium red bell peppers, roasted and diced
2	garlic cloves, minced
2/3	cup cooked long-grain rice
1/2	cup grated Parmesan cheese
1	large egg, lightly beaten
1/4	cup shredded basil leaves
1/4	teaspoon salt
	Freshly ground pepper
	Butter for greasing the ramekins
	Breadcrumbs for sprinkling the ramekins

Preheat the oven to 375°F.

Heat the oil in a large skillet over medium heat. Add the onion and cook, stirring occasionally, until soft, about 5 minutes. Add the zucchini, peppers, and garlic and cook, stirring, until soft, 10 to 15 minutes. Stir in the rice, Parmesan, egg, and basil and season with salt and pepper.

Butter six 1-cup ramekins and sprinkle with breadcrumbs. Spoon the vegetable mixture into the ramekins, pressing out any air. Bake until firm and lightly puffed, about 20 minutes. Cool briefly before unmolding.

FOR THE GOLDEN TOMATO COULIS

2	tablespoons olive oil
1	garlic clove, smashed
3	medium yellow tomatoes, peeled, seeded, and diced
2	tablespoons shredded basil leaves
2	pinches salt
	Pinch of cayenne

Farmer Tim Stark

Place the olive oil in a skillet over medium heat and add the garlic. Cook, stirring, until fragrant and golden, about 2 minutes. Stir in the tomatoes and simmer 5 minutes. Remove the garlic and puree the tomatoes in a blender or food processor. Stir in the basil and season with salt and cayenne.

To serve, unmold each tian in the center of a plate and spoon the sauce around.

ALAN TARDI

Roasted Autumn Vegetables

Chef Alan Tardi, of Follonico restaurant, urges you to choose the vegetables for this dish according to preference and availability. For the best visual effect and the best taste, use a variety of shapes, colors, and flavors.

To roast the vegetables below, you will need to use two baking sheets with sides (jelly-roll pans).

1	medium zucchini, quartered lengthwise and cut into $1^1/_2$-inch pieces
1	medium yellow squash, quartered lengthwise and cut into $1^1/_2$-inch pieces
3	carrots, peeled and cut into $1^1/_2$-inch pieces
1	pint red pearl onions, peeled
1	pint brussels sprouts, tough outer leaves removed, halved
6	small potatoes (preferably Yukon Gold), washed and halved
6	plum tomatoes, trimmed and halved
8	to 10 garlic cloves, peeled and smashed
3	tablespoons fresh thyme leaves (or 2 teaspoons dried)
$^1/_4$	cup roughly chopped fresh rosemary leaves (or 2 teaspoons dried)
	About 1 cup extra virgin olive oil
	Kosher salt and freshly ground pepper

Makes 8 appetizer or 4 main course servings

Preheat the oven to 500°F.

Toss each vegetable separately in a bowl with some of the garlic, herbs, olive oil (about 2 tablespoons of oil for each batch), salt, and pepper and place on a baking sheet. Begin roasting the carrots and potatoes and add the other vegetables as they are cooking. Roast until fork tender, removing each as it is done. Each vegetable will require a different amount of roasting time:

carrots, onions, and potatoes: 30 minutes

zucchini and yellow squash: 15 minutes

brussels sprouts: 12 minutes

tomatoes: 12 minutes

ALAN TARDI
Bagna Cauda

Chef Alan Tardi, a member of the Greenmarket advisory board, gives us his recipe for bagna cauda, a traditional dish from the Piemontese region of Italy. The light, garlicky sauce becomes a "hot bath" for all these wonderful vegetables, some cooked, some uncooked, all fresh and sweet.

2   bulbs garlic (about 5 ounces), peeled and sliced
2   cups olive oil, preferably extra virgin
3   anchovy filets, drained and quartered
1   teaspoon butter
     Pinch kosher salt
1   celery heart, cut into thin 2- to 3-inch sticks, with leaves
1   large beet, roasted or simmered; peeled, halved, and thinly sliced
1   head broccoli, cut into florets, blanched, shocked in cold water, and drained
2   bell peppers (1 red, 1 yellow), stemmed, seeded, and cut into 1-inch triangles
1   head romaine lettuce, tender inside leaves only
     Slices of crusty bread (optional, see note)
1   large egg, beaten (optional, see note)

Makes 4 to 6
appetizer servings

Place the garlic and olive oil in a heavy saucepan over medium-low heat. Bring to a simmer, stirring occasionally to prevent the garlic from sticking. Reduce the heat to low and continue to cook gently. Simmer until the garlic softens and begins to break down, about 35 minutes. Add the anchovies and simmer until they begin to disintegrate, about 5 minutes. Stir in the butter and season with salt.

To serve: Place the warm garlic dip in a bagna cauda dish, a fondue pot, or a small chafing dish with a candle underneath. Place on a large platter. Arrange the vegetables in a decorative fashion around the bagna cauda dish and serve. The lighted candle will keep the sauce warm.

Note: after most of the garlic sauce has been eaten, an egg is traditionally scrambled into the remaining hot sauce, and the mixture is scooped up with slices of bread.

BENITA MIGLIORELLI
Broccoli Rabe alla Migliorelli

Farmer Ken Migliorelli passed his mother Benita's recipe on to me. He and his wife, Mary Ellen, prepare this family favorite a few times a week during the fall months.

Broccoli rabe, sometimes sold as rapini, is a somewhat bitter and spicy green. A not-so-distant cousin of the familiar broccoli, it is more related to the turnip family, and at first glance may appear to be turnip greens, but upon close inspection, you will find little broccoli-like florets attached to the stalks. The Migliorellis save their own broccoli rabe seeds for replanting each year.

2	bunches broccoli rabe (about 4 pounds)
1/4	cup olive oil
6	large garlic cloves, peeled and chopped
3/4	teaspoon salt
1/4	to 1/2 teaspoon crushed red pepper

Makes 4 servings

Bring a large pot of water to a boil. Meanwhile, cut off the bottom 1/4 inch of the broccoli rabe stems and discard. Discard any yellow or brown leaves.

Add the greens to the hot water and simmer for 5 minutes. Drain in a colander; rinse with cold running water until cool, then cut into bite-size pieces.

Heat the olive oil in the pot over medium-low heat, add the garlic, salt, and crushed red pepper, and cook for 2 minutes. Add the broccoli rabe. Stir everything together, cover, and cook until heated through and tender, at least 5 and up to 30 minutes, depending on your taste.

VARIATIONS:

You may add Italian-style sausage, to taste, such as the sausage with fennel sold at Greenmarket by farmer Ted Blew. Allow the sausage to come to room temperature, then cut or tear into bite-size pieces. Before sautéeing the garlic, heat a tablespoon of olive oil in the pan over medium heat and add the sausage. When it has browned, remove it from the pan and continue the recipe, as above. When the broccoli rabe is cooked to a desired doneness, add the sausage and cook until heated through. You also may combine some of the reserved blanching water with the broccoli rabe and a pound of your favorite cooked pasta. Top off the dish with some fresh or aged goat cheese, such as those available at Greenmarket's Little Rainbow Chèvre or Coach Dairy Goat Farm. Or try golden raisins and a dash of balsamic vinegar.

JACK RIZZITELLO
Breaded Cauliflower

At the Saturday market, Marry and I often have the pleasure of chatting with Jack and his friend Bill, who carry many shopping bags that arrive empty but always leave full. Jack shared this simple, delicious fall recipe with us.

1   medium head cauliflower, separated into florettes
2   large eggs
2   tablespoons breadcrumbs
4   tablespoons grated Parmesan cheese
1/2 teaspoon salt
1/4 teaspoon freshly ground pepper
2   garlic cloves, smashed
2   tablespoons olive oil

Makes 4 to 6 servings

Wash the cauliflower sections in cold, salted water and rinse. Cook in a steamer over simmering water until just fork tender, about 5 minutes. Rinse with cold water until cool.

In a large bowl, beat together the eggs, breadcrumbs, and 2 tablespoons of the Parmesan cheese. Add the salt and pepper. Add the cauliflower and fold in with a rubber spatula.

In a large, nonstick skillet over medium heat, cook the garlic in the oil for 2 minutes, until golden. Remove the garlic and discard. Add the coated florets to the pan and cook over medium-high heat, turning occasionally, until golden brown on all sides, about 6 minutes.

Transfer to a serving dish and sprinkle with the remaining Parmesan.

ILENE ROSEN
Marinated Kermit Eggplants with Japanese Flavors

Chef de Cuisine Ilene Rosen of The City Bakery tells us that Kermits are Asian-style small eggplants that don't get much bigger than a tennis ball, if they get that big. They are a very pretty, variegated green, running from light to dark. This is a balanced, sweet, and pungent dish.

FOR THE JAPANESE VINAIGRETTE

- 1/4 cup Japanese rice vinegar
- 1/4 cup mirin (sweet rice wine)
- 1/4 cup vegetable oil
- 3 tablespoons soy sauce
- 2 garlic cloves, minced
- 2 tablespoons sake, optional

Makes 4 servings
(as a side dish)

In a large bowl, whisk together all the ingredients.

FOR THE EGGPLANT

- 4 Kermit eggplants, stems on (or substitute other small eggplants)

Cut an *X* in the bottom of each eggplant, extending up to the stem cap, cutting through the flesh to almost quarter the eggplant, but leaving it attached at the stem. Add the eggplants to the vinaigrette and marinate about 20 minutes, tossing several times.

Preheat the oven to 350°F. Place the eggplants on a baking sheet with sides, reserving the marinade. Roast the eggplants until soft, 30 to 40 minutes. Toss with the reserved marinade and then drain. Serve warm or at room temperature.

WAYNE NISH

Fricassee of Fish and Shellfish with Wild Mushrooms and Braised Greens

Chef Wayne Nish of March restaurant tells us that there are no wrong greens for this dish—use the best available fall greens of all varieties. In the spring, try mâche, baby beet greens, pea shoots, and mizuna; in the winter look for red kale, chard, and mustard greens.

1	cup chicken, fish, or vegetable stock
1/4	cup extra virgin olive oil
4	cups packed mixed greens, cleaned and torn
1	cup small whole wild mushrooms, or larger mushrooms, sliced
6	small littleneck clams, cleaned
6	mussels, cleaned
1/4	pound medium shrimp, shelled
1/4	pound large scallops
1/4	pound halibut, cod, or other white-fleshed fish
	Salt and freshly ground pepper

Makes 2 servings

Combine the stock, olive oil, and greens in a 10-inch skillet with a lid and bring to a boil. Add the mushrooms and let cook over high heat until the greens are softened and the stock is reduced by half, about 2 minutes.

Add the clams and mussels, cover, and cook 3 minutes. Add the remaining seafood, cover, and cook, shaking the pan once or twice until the mussels and clams have opened and the halibut is barely done, about 4 minutes. Season with pepper, and salt, if desired, and place the cooked greens and mushrooms in the center of 2 dinner plates or large shallow bowls. Arrange the seafood around the greens. Pour the juices from the pan on and around the greens and seafood.

NINA MELEDANDRI

Thanksgiving Lasagna

Nina is an outstanding painter and longtime family friend, who is almost a fixture at Greenmarket and has been on a first-name basis with many farmers for almost a decade.

This all-vegetable lasagna is one of her favorite recipes.

1	sugar pumpkin, about 2 pounds, halved lengthwise; or one 15-ounce can pumpkin
2	pounds fresh ricotta cheese
3	pounds fresh spinach, stemmed
6	tablespoons unsalted butter or olive oil, plus more for greasing the pan
1	Spanish onion (such as Ailsa Craig), finely chopped
$1\frac{1}{4}$	teaspoons salt
$\frac{3}{4}$	teaspoon freshly ground pepper
2	pinches nutmeg
$\frac{1}{3}$	cup all-purpose flour
$2\frac{1}{2}$	cups milk
2	large garlic cloves, minced
$1\frac{1}{2}$	pounds mixed mushrooms, such as cremini and shiitake, stemmed if necessary and quartered or diced
1	pound instant (no boil) lasagna noodles
$\frac{1}{4}$	cup freshly grated Parmesan cheese, plus more for serving
1	pound buffalo mozzarella or salted fresh mozzarella, thinly sliced

Makes 12 servings

Preheat the oven to 400°F. Place the pumpkin, cut sides down, on a baking sheet with sides. Roast for 1 hour. Let cool, discard the seeds, scoop out the flesh, and mash in a large bowl until smooth. Stir in the ricotta. Reserve.

Wash the spinach well, drain lightly in a colander, then place in a large pot. Cover and steam over high heat, stirring once or twice until wilted, about 5 minutes. Drain and rinse under cold water until cool. Squeeze the spinach firmly in batches to remove excess moisture, then coarsely chop. Set aside.

In a large saucepan over medium heat, melt 3 tablespoons of the butter. Add the onion and cook, stirring occasionally, until soft, about 8 minutes. Transfer half of the onion to the bowl with the pumpkin, $\frac{1}{4}$ teaspoon of the salt, $\frac{1}{8}$ teaspoon of the pepper, and the nutmeg, and stir to blend. Set aside.

Place the saucepan with the remaining onion over medium-high heat. Stir in

1 tablespoon of butter, then the flour, to make a paste; cook, stirring, for 1 minute. Gradually whisk in the milk, then continue whisking until hot and thick, about 8 minutes. Season with ½ teaspoon of the salt and ⅛ teaspoon of the pepper. Remove ⅔ cup of the white sauce and reserve. Stir the cooked spinach into the remaining sauce in the pot and set aside.

In a medium skillet over medium heat, melt the remaining 2 tablespoons of butter. Add the garlic and cook, stirring until golden, about 2 minutes. Add the mushrooms, season with ½ teaspoon each of salt and pepper, and cook, stirring occasionally, until nicely browned, about 10 minutes.

Grease a 15 by 10 by 3-inch baking dish. Add the reserved ⅔ cup of white sauce and tilt the pan to coat. Add one layer of lasagna noodles, breaking a sheet if necessary to fill the pan; take care not to let the pasta touch the sides of the pan, or it will not cook properly. Spread half of the pumpkin mixture on top. Cover with another layer of noodles, then half of the spinach, then more noodles. Spoon all of the cooked mushrooms on top; sprinkle with 2 tablespoons of the Parmesan and top with half of the mozzarella. Repeat layering with noodles, the remaining spinach, the remaining pumpkin, and ending with noodles.

Place the remaining mozzarella and 2 tablespoons Parmesan on top. Pour 1 cup of water around the edge of the pasta. Cover snugly with foil and bake for 1 hour. Uncover and bake for 15 minutes. Let stand for 20 minutes. Cut and serve.

Farmer Stanley
Osczepinski

SCOTT CAMPBELL

New England Pumpkin Puree with Pan-Roasted Sea Scallops

Chef Scott Campbell has an ongoing and steady commitment to local farms and brings that commitment to his menu at Avenue Restaurant. Here he combines scallops, one of my favorite things from the sea, and pumpkin into a perfect fall treat.

FOR THE PUMPKIN

- 1 small pumpkin, quartered and seeded (or 2 butternut squash), about 2 pounds total
- 2 tablespoons butter
- 1 teaspoon kosher salt
  Freshly ground pepper

Makes 4 servings

Preheat the oven to 400°F. Place the pumpkin on a baking sheet and roast until very soft, 1 to 1½ hours. Peel and puree in a food processor. Transfer to a bowl. Stir in the butter, salt, and pepper. Keep warm, covered, in a low oven, or reheat later in a microwave. (Makes 3 cups puree.)

FOR THE BEURRE BLANC

- 1 tablespoon chopped shallots
- 3 tablespoons dry white wine
- ¼ cup clam juice
- 2 tablespoons water
- 4 tablespoons butter
- ⅛ teaspoon salt
  Freshly ground pepper

Combine the shallots, wine, clam juice, and water in a medium saucepan over medium-high heat. Boil until reduced to ⅓ total volume, about 5 minutes. Stir in the butter. Season with the salt and pepper to taste.

FOR THE SCALLOPS

- 3 tablespoons butter
- 1½ pounds sea scallops, muscle removed
- ¼ teaspoon kosher salt
- Freshly ground pepper

In a large pan over medium-high heat, heat the butter until brown and cook the scallops until golden brown, turning once, about 5 minutes. Season with salt and pepper.

TO ASSEMBLE

- 2 plum tomatoes, finely diced
- 6 sprigs thyme
- 3 tablespoons minced chives.

Divide the warm pumpkin puree among 4 bowls and top each with 8 scallops. Spoon the sauce over, and sprinkle the tomatoes, thyme, and chives on top.

Playing on the pumpkins

LLOYD FEIT
Sautéed Skate Wing with Kale and Hot Pepper Beurre Blanc

Lloyd Feit's Café Loup is a traditional French bistro on West Thirteenth Street, a few blocks from Greenmarket. Bistro is an overused word these days, but Lloyd was "bistroing" fifteen or twenty years ago, long before anyone else. Customers comment on his beautiful art collection and his authentic French food.

Although you can find skate year-round, Lloyd serves it with kale on his winter and fall menus.

FOR THE KALE

2	tablespoons vegetable oil
6	garlic cloves, peeled and finely chopped
4	large heads kale (about 5 pounds), trimmed, rinsed, and roughly chopped
1/4	cup soy sauce
1/4	cup chicken stock
1/2	teaspoon sugar
1/4	tablespoon salt
1/4	tablespoon freshly ground pepper
	Few drops sesame oil

Makes 6 servings

Heat the vegetable oil in a wok over high heat, add the garlic, and stir fry for 1 minute until golden. Add the kale, soy sauce, chicken stock, sugar, salt, and pepper and cook, stirring until wilted, about 5 minutes. Sprinkle with sesame oil. Keep warm.

FOR THE HOT PEPPER BEURRE BLANC

1/2	cup dry white wine, such as Chardonnay or Sauvignon Blanc
1/4	cup finely chopped shallots (2 medium shallots)
2	sticks (1/2 pound) butter, softened
1/2	teaspoon salt
	Freshly ground pepper
1	serrano or jalapeño chile, very thinly sliced

Combine the wine and shallots in a small saucepan over high heat. Boil until very reduced and almost dry. Remove from the heat, slowly whisk in the butter, and season with salt and pepper. Strain through a fine sieve and stir in the sliced chile. Keep warm.

FOR THE SKATE WING

1/2	cup milk
6	skinned skate wing fillets (4 to 6 ounces each)
3/4	cup flour
1/4	teaspoon salt
	Freshly ground pepper
1/3	cup vegetable oil or olive oil

In a large bowl, pour the milk over the skate. Cover and refrigerate for 30 minutes. Remove the fish from the milk, toss together the flour, salt, and pepper, and coat the fish fillets in the flour.

Heat the oil in a large skillet over medium-high heat. Cook the skate in batches, until nicely golden on both sides, about 5 minutes, turning once.

Divide the kale among 6 dinner plates. Place the skate on top and drizzle with the beurre blanc.

JOYCE QUATTROCIOCCHI
Roasted Wild Turkey with Bread Stuffing

Quattro's Game Farm has been raising game for three generations. Joyce, who comes from the Migliorelli farming family, farther up the Hudson Valley, married Sal Quattrociocchi, so this is a true market-farm marriage.

Wild turkey isn't overly gamey, as some might expect—it is rich and flavorful. You can make the stuffing and stock ahead of time in order to cut down on preparation on the day you want to serve the turkey.

Make sure the stuffing is cool or cold before stuffing the turkey. Never stuff a bird with hot stuffing!

FOR THE TURKEY STOCK

Neck, heart, and gizzard from one 7- to 8-pound wild turkey
(do not use the liver)

Makes 6 servings

2 1/2	cups water
1/2	stalk celery, cut in 2 pieces
1/2	carrot, peeled and cut in 2 pieces
1/2	small onion, peeled

Combine all ingredients for the stock in a saucepan over medium heat and simmer 30 to 45 minutes. Strain. (This can be made up to 1 day ahead. Let cool completely, cover, and refrigerate. Skim off any fat before using.)

FOR THE BREAD STUFFING

2	tablespoons unsalted butter
1	large onion, finely chopped
3	large celery ribs, finely chopped
1	2-pound loaf white sandwich bread (or half white and half whole wheat) cut into 1/2-inch dice
2	cups turkey or chicken stock (or 1 cup broth and 1 cup water)
2	large eggs, beaten
1/2	cup milk
2	tablespoons finely chopped fresh sage
1/2	teaspoon dried thyme
3/4	teaspoon salt
1/4	teaspoon freshly ground pepper

Melt the butter in a medium skillet over medium-low heat. Add the onion and celery and cook, stirring often, until translucent, about 10 minutes. Let cool.

Transfer the onion mixture to a large bowl with the bread, stock, eggs, milk, sage, thyme, salt, and pepper. Mix with your hands until well blended. Let the stuffing cool completely before stuffing the turkey (it can be covered and refrigerated up to 3 days).

Stuff the mixture into the cavity of the turkey without packing tightly. Stuff the neck cavity, then if necessary, place any remaining stuffing in a baking dish. (Bake the stuffing beside the turkey for 1 hour.)

FOR THE TURKEY

1	wild turkey, 7 to 8 pounds, giblets and neck reserved for turkey stock
	Bread stuffing
1	large onion, thinly sliced
1	tablespoon butter, melted
1/4	teaspoon salt
1/4	teaspoon freshly ground black pepper

Preheat the oven to 450°F.

Rinse the turkey well with cold water. Pull out and trim excess fat from the cavity and neck end and discard. Stuff and truss the turkey. Arrange the sliced onion over the bottom of a roasting pan large enough to accommodate the turkey, and place the turkey on top, breast side up. Brush with the melted butter and season with the salt and pepper. Roast in the oven for 45 minutes.

Pour 1 cup water in the pan, for basting later. Lower the temperature to 350°F, cover the turkey with foil, and roast about 2½ hours longer, basting every 30 minutes, until the internal temperature is 180°F on an instant-read thermometer inserted into the thigh and stuffing, the juices run clear, and the drumstick wiggles loosely.

Graham Hawks of Keith's
Organic Farm

FOR THE GRAVY

Pan juices

1½   cups chicken or turkey stock,
or ³/₄ cup broth and ³/₄ cup water

2   tablespoons all-purpose flour

¼   cup cold water

¼   cup sherry or white wine

¼   teaspoon salt

Freshly ground pepper

When the turkey is done, remove it from the pan and set aside. Pour the pan juices into a bowl and skim off as much of the fat as possible, reserving about ¼ cup. Add the stock to the pan juices.

In a small bowl, whisk together the flour and the cold water; add to the roasting pan with the stock and pan juices. Place over medium heat, stir in the sherry, and bring to a boil. Simmer for 5 minutes, stirring frequently, until thickened. Season with salt and pepper.

ERICA DE MANE

Lamb Stew with Butternut Squash and Rosemary

In this recipe from cookbook author and market customer Erica De Mane, the squash mellows and thickens the stew, taking the place of potatoes, which are more commonly used in similar dishes. You can also try this with pumpkin or yams. The stew is delicious served with baked rice or a small pasta, such as orzo.

Greenmarkets are good sources for naturally, often organically raised, meats of excellent quality, such as lamb.

Makes 6 servings

1/4	cup olive oil, plus more if needed
4	pounds boneless, trimmed lamb shoulder or leg, cut into 1 1/2-inch chunks
3/4	teaspoon salt
2	large onions, cut into medium dice
3	cloves garlic, minced
1	cup dry white wine
3	cups chicken stock (see Greenmarket Pantry), or low-salt canned broth
2	bay leaves
3	sprigs rosemary, 2 left whole and 1 with leaves chopped
2	ripe tomatoes, seeded and chopped
1	small butternut squash, peeled, seeded, and cut into 1/2-inch cubes
	Freshly ground black pepper

In a large heavy casserole with a lid, heat 2 tablespoons of the olive oil over medium-high heat. Add half the lamb, season it with 1/4 teaspoon of the salt, and brown it well on all sides, about 8 minutes. Transfer it to a plate and repeat with the remaining oil and meat.

Add the onions to the pot and cook, stirring, until they just start to soften, about 5 minutes. Add the garlic and cook 1 minute more.

Add the wine and let it bubble a few minutes to cook out some of the alcohol. Add the meat stock, bay leaves, and whole rosemary sprigs and bring to a boil. Reduce the heat to low, add the tomatoes, cover the pan, and simmer 2 hours. (This can be made to this point 1 day ahead. Let cool completely and refrigerate overnight. Rewarm before continuing.)

Skim off the excess fat and remove the bay leaves and rosemary sprigs. Add the squash and chopped rosemary and cook until both the lamb and the squash are very tender, about 20 minutes. Season with the remaining salt and pepper to taste. If the stew gets very thick after the squash is cooked, add a bit more stock or water.

BILL TELEPAN

Veal, Celery Root, Wild Mushrooms, and Gremolata with Egg Noodles

This stick-to-your-ribs dish from a celebrated chef brings together the richness of farm-fresh veal, the deep flavor of wild mushrooms, and the lightness of herbs. Earthy celery root appears both in the stew and as a crunchy garnish. Serve this with homemade or store-bought pasta.

Makes 4 servings

$3/4$	cup white wine
$1/2$	carrot, scrubbed and thinly sliced
1	small onion, peeled and thinly sliced
1	rib celery, thinly sliced
3	garlic cloves, smashed
1	sprig thyme
4	slices veal shank (about 1 inch thick each; about $2^{1}/_{2}$ pounds)
$1^{1}/_{2}$	cups chicken stock or water (or a mixture of half water and half stock)
1	medium celery root (about 10 ounces), peeled and halved
1	small russet potato (about 2 ounces), peeled
$1/4$	cup plus 2 tablespoons heavy cream
	Salt and freshly ground pepper
2	tablespoons unsalted butter
8	ounces shiitake mushrooms, stemmed and sliced thin
	Zest of 1 lemon, grated
$1^{1}/_{2}$	tablespoons finely chopped herbs, such as chives, parsley, rosemary, and thyme, or a combination
1	pound egg noodles, cooked and drained, for serving

Combine the wine, carrot, onion, celery, garlic, and thyme in a large bowl. Add the veal and turn. Cover and refrigerate for 8 hours or overnight.

Remove the veal from the marinade. Place the wine mixture in a large saucepan and bring to a boil. Reduce the heat and simmer for 5 minutes. Pour in the stock. Return the veal to the pot, cover, and simmer very gently until the veal is tender, $1\frac{1}{2}$ to 2 hours.

Meanwhile, bring a small saucepan of salted water to a boil. Cut 1 piece of the celery root and the potato into $\frac{1}{4}$-inch chunks. Add to the water and cook

until tender, about 15 minutes. Drain and mash well. Stir in the cream. Reserve.

Remove the cooked veal and set aside to cool slightly. Return the liquid to a boil and reduce to 1½ cups, about 15 minutes. Whisk in the celery root mixture and bring to a boil; then remove from the heat. Strain through a fine strainer, pressing down on the solids. Break the veal into bite-size pieces and add to the sauce with ½ teaspoon salt and ¼ teaspoon pepper.

Melt 1 tablespoon of the butter in a large skillet over high heat. Add the mushrooms and cook, stirring occasionally, until browned, about 6 minutes. Stir into the veal mixture. Cut the second piece of celery root into ⅓-inch dice. Melt the remaining 1 tablespoon of butter in the skillet, add the celery root, and cook until golden and tender, about 8 minutes. Stir into the veal mixture and adjust seasoning, if necessary.

To make the gremolata, combine the lemon zest and chopped herbs in a small bowl.

Place the cooked noodles in 4 warm bowls, spoon the veal mixture over, and sprinkle with the gremolata. Serve immediately.

PETER IVY

Lamb Carnitas and Toasted Cumin with Angel-Hair Pasta

Truth be told, I had to ask what carnitas were, when Chef Peter Ivy gave me this recipe, and I learned that they are crisply roasted little cubes of savory meat. Lamb cubes are used in this dish, roasted with garlic, onion, cumin, and chile pepper. They make an unusual, tasty sauce for pasta, one that our recipe tester rated a double thumbs up!

FOR THE LAMB

2	pounds boneless leg of lamb, cut into $1/2$-inch dice
$1/4$	cup corn oil
4	garlic cloves, minced
1	jalapeño pepper, minced
1	onion, halved and thinly sliced
1	tablespoon chili powder, preferably ancho
$1/8$	teaspoon salt
	Freshly ground pepper

Makes 6 servings

Preheat the oven to 450°F. In a mixing bowl, combine the lamb with the oil, garlic, pepper, onion, and chili powder. Season with salt and pepper to taste.

Spread the lamb on a baking sheet and roast until lightly crisped, 15 to 20 minutes.

FOR THE PASTA

1	pound angel-hair pasta
2	tablespoons cumin seeds
1	cup packed cilantro leaves, coarsely chopped
2	scallions, thinly sliced
6	plum tomatoes, seeded and finely diced
	Salt and freshly ground pepper

Bring a large pot of salted water to a boil and cook the pasta until al dente. Drain and let cool. Transfer to a large bowl.

Meanwhile, in a small dry skillet over medium-low heat, toast the cumin, shaking the pan until fragrant, 2 to 3 minutes. Let cool.

Add the cumin seeds, cilantro, scallions, and tomatoes to the pasta and season with salt and pepper. Top with the lamb and serve.

DAVID HILL

Pork Chops Braised in Hard Cider

David Hill is a longtime Greenmarket customer, originally from England, who gives us an English way to cook pork chops, in this simple and straightforward recipe. Mashed potatoes are a good accompaniment for these juicy chops.

Although hard cider isn't sold at the Union Square Greenmarket, you can find it in wine and liquor shops.

Makes 4 servings

2 tablespoons olive oil
4 medium onions, thinly sliced
3 red bell peppers, stemmed, seeded, and thinly sliced
1 bay leaf
4 boneless pork chops
$1/4$ teaspoon salt
$1/4$ teaspoon freshly ground pepper
1 cup hard cider

Heat the oil in a large skillet over medium-high heat. Add the onions to the skillet and cook, stirring often, until golden brown, about 4 minutes. Add the bell peppers and bay leaf and cook over medium-low heat until the peppers are soft, about 7 minutes. Season the chops with the salt and pepper, then add to the pan. Cook, turning once, until nicely browned on both sides, about 6 minutes. Add the cider and simmer gently, turning occasionally, until the chops are cooked through, about 8 minutes more. Remove the bay leaf, adjust seasoning if necessary, and serve.

TONY AND CHRISTINE MANNETTA

Chorizo Chili

Tony Mannetta, director of the Greenmarket, and his wife, Christine, suggest that you serve this chili with your favorite corn bread smeared with Beth's Farm Kitchen's Mighty Hot Pepper Jelly, available at Greenmarket. Or use any hot pepper jelly of your choice.

8	links chorizo sausage, preferably from High Hope Hogs Farm (about 2 pounds), quartered lengthwise and sliced $1/4$ inch thick crosswise
1	large yellow onion, chopped
$1/2$	teaspoon chili powder, or to taste
$1/2$	teaspoon ground cumin
4	large cloves garlic, minced
1	green bell pepper, chopped medium
1	jalapeño pepper, finely diced
2	cups seeded and diced plum tomatoes (1 pound)
1	cup fresh corn kernels
2	cups cooked black beans (or a 19-ounce can, drained)
1	cup water
$1/4$	cup dark or amber beer
1	bay leaf

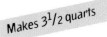

Makes $3^1/2$ quarts

In a Dutch oven, brown the sausage 10 minutes, and remove. Add the onion, chili powder, and cumin and sauté until the onion is soft, about 8 minutes. Add the garlic, bell pepper, and jalapeño and sauté until soft, 5 minutes more. Add the tomatoes, corn, beans, water, beer, and bay leaf; return the sausage to the Dutch oven, and bring almost to a boil. Reduce the heat and simmer $1/2$ hour. Remove the bay leaf.

Serve in bowls, accompanied by corn bread and hot pepper jelly.

CONNIE McCABE
Poached Quince Two Ways

Enthusiastic Greenmarket customer Connie McCabe says: "I never knew a quince until I discovered Locust Grove Farms. Since then, I have been hooked and I have made it a crusade to introduce unsuspecting, unfamiliar market customers to the fruit. I love baking and stewing quince, but for company, poaching is the way to go."

FOR THE QUINCE
4   quince, about 10 ounces each

Peel the quince and discard the peels. Put the peeled quince in a bowl of water and lemon juice to prevent browning.

FOR THE WINE POACHING LIQUID
1   bottle dry white wine
1   cup water
1/2   cup sugar
1/2   vanilla pod, split lengthwise and beans scraped out
3   sprigs tarragon

Makes 4 servings

FOR THE HONEY POACHING LIQUID
3   cups water
1   cup honey
     Juice and zest (yellow part only) of 2 lemons
12   cloves

Place the quince in a saucepan big enough to hold them in a single layer. Add the ingredients for either the wine poaching or honey poaching liquid. Bring the poaching mixture to a simmer. Cook the quince, turning occasionally, until tender, about 30 minutes. Let the quince cool completely in the poaching liquid. Remove the quince from the liquid, quarter, and core. Place in a bowl. Meanwhile, bring the other poaching liquid to a boil and reduce until syrupy, about 15 minutes. Let cool, then strain over the quince. Serve at room temperature.

WALTER AND NONI BAUER
Honey-Caramel Apples

Walter and Noni Bauer maintain 800 bee colonies—houses of bees—and they are honey experts. This simple, traditional fall recipe, a treat for Thanksgiving or Halloween, is one of Noni's favorites.

8	Popsicle sticks
8	small, tart apples, such as Mutsu
2	cups honey
$3/4$	cup evaporated milk
1	teaspoon vanilla
3	tablespoons butter
$1/4$	teaspoon salt

Makes 8 servings

Oil a large baking sheet and set aside. Insert a stick into each apple.

In a saucepan over medium heat, cook the honey and milk, stirring constantly, to the firm ball stage, 255°F on a candy thermometer, about 10 minutes. Stir in the vanilla, butter, and salt.

Dip the apples one at a time into the caramel and cover evenly. Place on the baking sheet and chill until set.

James Kent and Sawyer

JOEL PATRAKER

Marry and Joel's Applesauce

Homemade applesauce is like mashed potatoes—everyone likes it a different way. Should it be chunky or smooth, natural, sweetened, or flavored? Marry and I make applesauce every fall with beautiful Greenmarket apples, and each batch is different.

4	pounds apples, a mixture of large and small varieties (such as McIntosh, Jonagold, Jonathan, Tydeman's Early Red, Sweet Sixteen, Gala, Eve's Delight)
1/4	cup water, plus more as needed
2	tablespoons brown sugar (or maple syrup)
1	tablespoon fresh lemon juice
1/2	teaspoon ground ginger
1/2	teaspoon ground cinnamon

Makes about 2 quarts

Peel, quarter, and core the apples, then cut the quarters in half. (You can leave the peels on a few of the most fragrant apples for extra fragrance and flavor.)

Combine the apples and water in a large saucepan and simmer, partially covered, over medium heat until the apples are tender, about 45 minutes, stirring occasionally to prevent the apples from sticking.

Stir in the brown sugar or maple syrup, lemon juice, ginger, and cinnamon.

Run the apples through a food mill or, to keep the texture somewhat chunky, mash with a potato masher. Remove any peels before serving.

Serve warm or chilled. Can be refrigerated, tightly covered, up to 1 week.

The tired home cook

MARY CLEAVER
Pear Crisp

This homey dessert from The Cleaver Company, a fine local caterer, reminds me of the beloved cobblers and crisps of my childhood. I was always more than willing to trade a few entrees and side dishes in the school cafeteria for a serving of one of these fruity, crumbly treats.

The recipe can be cut in half and baked in a 9 by 9-inch pan.

FOR THE PEARS

12	firm pears, such as Bartlett or Bosc, peeled, cored, and cut into pieces
1/4	cup fresh lemon juice
	2-inch-long piece fresh ginger, grated
1	cup flour
1½	cups sugar

Makes 12 to 16 servings

Preheat the oven to 350°F. Lightly grease a 3-quart shallow baking dish or gratin, or a 13 by 9-inch baking dish.

Place the pears in a large bowl, add the lemon juice, and sprinkle the grated ginger on top. Add the flour and sugar. Gently toss the fruit to evenly mix the ingredients. Spoon into the prepared baking dish.

FOR THE TOPPING

1/2	pound (2 sticks) unsalted butter
2/3	cup honey, preferably wildflower
4	cups rolled oats
1½	cups all-purpose flour
1	cup coarsely chopped pecans
2	teaspoons cinnamon
1	teaspoon ground ginger
1	teaspoon salt

Melt together the butter and honey in a small saucepan over low heat. In a large bowl, stir together the oats, flour, pecans, cinnamon, ginger, and salt. Add the honey-butter to the bowl and stir until evenly blended.

Spread the topping evenly over the pears and bake, uncovered, until the top is well browned and the fruit is bubbling, 40 to 45 minutes.

DAVID TURK

Pumpkin Crème Brûlée

This is a variation on a classic from Chef David Turk, of Indiana Market and Catering, and it is quite a treat. You can easily make it at home, using your broiler to achieve a crisp crust. Of course, the heavy cream comes from Greenmarket, as does the pumpkin, but in a pinch you can substitute pumpkin from a can.

4	large eggs
1½	cups heavy cream
½	cup cooked and pureed fresh pumpkin, or use canned
¼	cup sugar, plus more for sprinkling
¼	teaspoon salt
½	teaspoon powdered ginger
½	teaspoon cinnamon

Makes 6 servings

Preheat the oven to 300°F.

In a mixing bowl, whisk together the eggs, cream, pumpkin, sugar, salt, ginger, and cinnamon.

Place six 6-ounce ramekins in a shallow roasting pan. Pour the egg mixture into the ramekins, filling to ½ inch from the top. Pour hot water into the pan to come halfway up the ramekins. Bake until the mixture is set, but still a little wobbly, about 1 hour. Remove from the pan, let cool for 1 hour, then refrigerate until well chilled, 2 hours or up to 24 hours.

To finish the custards, preheat the broiler. Sprinkle about 1 teaspoon of sugar over the top of each ramekin. Run under the hot broiler until melted and caramelized, about 30 seconds. Watch carefully so the sugar does not burn. Serve at once.

MAURY RUBIN
Indian Apple Pie

In the morning, you see Maury Rubin and his kitchen crew shopping with the other chefs and customers for the best fruit offered by Greenmarket farmers. This superb homespun pie, a cross between Indian pudding and apple pie, will be a surprise for Maury's fans, who have come to expect minimalist tarts from The City Bakery in Manhattan.

FOR THE TOPPING
- 3/4 cup light brown sugar
- 1/2 cup all-purpose flour
- 1/4 cup coarse cornmeal
- 1 teaspoon cinnamon
- 4 tablespoons unsalted butter, cut into 1/2-inch pieces
- 1 1/2 tablespoons heavy cream

Makes one 9-inch pie, 6 to 8 servings

Place the brown sugar, flour, cornmeal, and cinnamon in a large bowl and toss together well. Add the butter and rub it into the mixture with your fingertips to form peasize lumps. Using a butter knife, stir in the cream until incorporated.

FOR THE FILLING
- 4 tablespoons unsalted butter, softened
- 2 tablespoons sugar
- 1/2 cup milled unsulphured molasses
- 2 teaspoons all-purpose flour
- 1 1/2 teaspoons cinnnamon
- 1/2 teaspoon ground ginger
- 2 pounds Rome or Cortland apples, peeled, halved, cored, and cut into 12 wedges each

In a large bowl, whisk together the butter, sugar, molasses, flour, cinnamon, and ginger until smooth. Add the apples and fold with a rubber spatula until well coated.

TO ASSEMBLE
One 9-inch piecrust (see page 16)

Preheat the oven to 375°F.

Spoon the apples into the piecrust. Spread the sticky topping over the apples (it will melt and cover most of them as it bakes).

Place the pie pan on a baking sheet, and place in the middle of the oven. Bake for 30 minutes, then cover loosely with foil and bake 30 to 40 minutes longer, until the apples are tender when pierced with a fork. Let cool about 20 minutes.

Helen Kent's Apple Pie

Helen is the matriarch of the Kent family of Locust Grove Orchards and her apple pie—as might be expected—is one of the most sought-after items in Greenmarket. Unfortunately, she doesn't have as much time as she used to for baking, so eager customers can't always buy one. But she has been kind enough to share her recipe for the pie of all pies. Try this topped with vanilla ice cream, for the classic apple pie à la mode.

Helen advises that Northern Spy apples are the best for pie. Since they take a long time to bake, slice them thinly. We tried Helen's recipe with a combination of Mutsu and Rome, and had great results.

FOR THE PIECRUST

1½	cups all-purpose flour
½	cup vegetable shortening
¼	teaspoon salt
1	large egg yolk, lightly beaten
5	tablespoons ice water

Makes one 9-inch pie, 6 to 8 servings

In a mixing bowl, combine the flour, shortening, and salt and mix until crumbly. Add the egg yolk and water and mix well until the dough comes together. Divide in half and form into 2 disks. Roll one piece out to an 11-inch circle. Fit into a 9-inch pie pan.

FOR THE APPLE PIE FILLING

3	pounds apples, peeled, quartered, cored, and sliced (6 to 7 cups; Northern Spy, Mutsu, Rome, or other good baking apples)
1	tablespoon fresh lemon juice (to keep the apples from turning brown)
1	teaspoon cinnamon
⅔	cup sugar
3	tablespoons flour
2	tablespoons unsalted butter cut into bits

Preheat the oven to 400°F.

In a large bowl, combine the apples and lemon juice. Sprinkle the cinnamon, sugar, and flour on top and toss to combine. Pile the apples into the pie shell and dot with the butter. Cover with the top crust and crimp the edges. Cut several vents in the top with a sharp knife tip.

Bake for 30 minutes; turn the oven down to 350°F and bake for another 30 to 45 minutes, until steam comes through the vents. Let cool at least 30 minutes before serving.

Winter

Common sense dictates that winter is the season least likely to provide a meal from the farmers' stands at Greenmarket. Gone are the summer heirloom tomatoes that caught our eye with their rich colors and skins bursting with juice. Fresh sweet corn has been replaced by cornmeal, and the only hot peppers are the ones a thoughtful farmer remembered to dry, back in September.

But the winter sunlight is bright and direct, even harsh; it gives the produce at the market an essential advantage. The light pink color of a Tiger Rose radish, the deep brown of a burdock root, the whiteness of a goat cheese, all stand out in this light. The remaining crimson apples and golden pears don't have to compete for attention with their brothers and sisters of the fall harvest. The choices are fewer and more easily defined.

On the farms, the same sunlight reaches the fields, now unprotected by the lush foliage of late summer. If a good snow cover comes before a hard frost, broccoli and other greens will grow beneath it to brighten our tables in early spring.

It's easy for city dwellers to forget that life on the farm goes on during the winter months. Cows, chickens, and lambs still must be fed, trees pruned, and greenhouses cared for. Farmers use their time indoors to study seed catalogues and review winning and losing crops from the past season. Is it worth taking a chance on a melon variety enjoyed by only a few customers? Will a crop show more promise if planted on ground with better drainage? Will the coming summer be drier than the last?

As the snow-covered fields rest, life in the city continues to move at a lightning-fast pace, with a steady flow, perhaps a torrent, of holiday meals and busy Greenmarket days. In December, Christmas tree growers arrive at the market, their beautiful displays forming a backdrop for the seasonal good-byes exchanged by departing farmers, market managers, and customers. Repeatedly, customers ask me where their favorite farmer or crop has

gone. Alas, there is no more fennel, and the heady perfume of ripe grapes can now be found only in juice or jam. Winter has moved ahead of our appetites.

Looking around the market on a brisk, sunny January morning, I notice how empty the aisles have become. The seventy stands that make up the Union Square Greenmarket have been reduced to twenty, spread out over the same area. Like a young child who has begun to lose baby teeth, Greenmarket has a smile that looks a little funny. But it is still too early to begin raiding the freezer for the summer produce that my wife, Marry, has frozen: the beans, tomatoes, pesto base, and blueberries that will keep us fed through February and March. Eating locally with the seasons can be challenging but the market doesn't close for the winter, and I can still stock my pantry with winter squash, carrots, radishes, rutabagas, leeks, parsnips, potatoes, beets, cider, honey, and maple syrup.

Later in the season, in February, I look at the

same scene and try to imagine what possible consolation I might give myself for being outside in this harsh weather. As I walk briskly along the aisles to keep warm and promote morale among the farmers, a chance encounter at Paf-

Linda Mac Claren of Whippoorwill Farms

fenroths' stand gives me a reason to consider the parsnip. The dusty roots are heaped haphazardly, overflowing the sides of a wooden crate that has failed to contain them.

Once the bold ruler of winter tables, the parsnip was dethroned by the potato. It is not a particularly exciting vegetable to behold, with its unremarkable color, large round shoulders, sunken neck, ringed body, and tapered bottom.

Washed twice—once when the farmer takes it from the field and once in your kitchen—it's still coated with light brown dust, a reminder of the soil in which it grew. But the parsnip, so often passed over for sexier fingerling potatoes or blood-red beets, for me, holds the secret of winter. I raise one to my nose and smell it. Its faint ethereal scent combines a little earth and a little carrot—just a hint of the wonder and magic contained within. My mind fills with the image of a warm kitchen and Marry and me cooking together. A horn blares, a bicyclist curses, and I am suddenly back at wintery Union Square. I take two large handfuls of parsnips and bring them to the scale to be weighed.

At home that evening, Marry isn't ready to share my enthusiasm for a dinner composed mostly of a root vegetable, but she joins me in the kitchen. We drink red wine to chase away the chill as we wash and peel the parsnips. We place them whole in a large baking dish with a little Ronnybrook Farm fresh butter, and cover the dish. As the parsnips bake in the oven, our apartment is filled with a warm, sweet, savory aroma that pushes the cold air back outside where it belongs.

As soon as the parsnips are tender enough to be pierced with a fork, I remove them from the baking dish and place them on a cutting board. I slice them crosswise from the bottom to the top, and the slices get thicker as I go. We stand in the kitchen eating butter-coated, hot parsnip slices, buttery juice running down our chins. We both smile with the realization that the parsnip, like winter itself, is all about simplicity and inner warmth. This staple, this seemingly unremarkable root vegetable has, with very little effort on our part, taken the chill from our bodies and our home, brought smiles to our faces, and renewed our connection with the seasons. All this for about eighty cents a pound!

Filling Your Market Basket in Winter
January, February, March

Blossoms
Pussy Willow

Cut Flowers
Rose
Assorted dried flowers

Potted Flowers
Lily
Hyacinth
Paperwhite
Iris

Freshly Cut Herbs
Rosemary
Sage
Thyme

Lettuce
Mixed Baby Lettuce

Salad and Cooking Greens
Microgreens

Spinach
Mâche

Vegetables
Brussels Sprouts
Cabbage (Red and Green)
Savoy Cabbage
Winter Squash

Root Crops
Shallot
Parsnip
Leek
Onion: Red Torpedo; White
    Bermuda; Cippolini;
    Ailsa Craig
Rutabaga
Turnip
Potato
Radish: Black; French
    Breakfast; Daikon;
    China Rose

Cultivated Mushrooms
Button
Cremini
Portobello
Shiitake

Eggs
Chicken
Duck
Goose
Pheasant
Wild Turkey
Guinea Hen

Poultry, Meat, and Game
Venison
Muscovy Duck
Pekin Duck
Pheasant
Partridge
Wild Turkey
Domestic Turkey
Goose

Guinea Hen
Capon
Quail
Wild Boar
Chicken

Fish and Seafood
Cod
Sea Scallop
Scrod (Hake)
Yellow Tail Flounder
Oysters
Clams

Also available in winter
    are dried grains, dried
    flowers and grasses;
    honey; maple syrup;
    prepared products,
    such as eggnog, jams,
    and cider; and seasonal
    baked goods, such as
    hearty breads.

Winter Recipes

Winter

MARKET PEOPLE
Jim Grillo

Jim Grillo, one-time county deputy sheriff, sometime painter, and full-time farmer, owns Northshire Farm in West Winfield, New York. He and his young son, Zach, raise game birds, hogs, chickens, rabbits, and lambs; and in the warmer months, some of the tastiest blueberries, muskmelons, and sweet potatoes I've ever eaten.

By the middle of February, all of Jim's fall harvest has been gobbled up by hungry New Yorkers. Then his market stand becomes a small butcher shop, with rows of packaged Canadian-style bacon neatly lined up next to rabbit and pork sausages, whole rab-

bits, poussins (very young, small chickens), and larger broiling and stewing chickens.

Jim decided one cold winter day that he wanted to entice passersby with the aromas of savory, steaming-hot food, and the best way to do that was to cook some chicken along with aromatic market vegetables. Using a large, stainless steel wok and a somewhat wobbly three-legged propane stove borrowed from his Greenmarket neighbors, Walter and Noni Bauer, he prepared a coq au vin, fragrant with garlic, onions, red wine, and herbs. His plan worked very well and hungry shoppers were drawn, oohing and aahing, to his stand. However, when any of them asked for a taste, Jim responded: "Sorry—this is for us! But I'll tell you how to make it at home." Which led Walter Bauer to dub him the Grouchy Gourmet.

Look for The Grouchy Gourmet's Coq au Vin on page 153. This is the recipe that will tell you how to make it at home.

Jim Grillo, "The Grouchy Gormet"

MARKET PEOPLE
Lynn and Charles Buck

Lynn and Charles Buck of Buck Hill Farm tap their acres of maple trees and process the sap to make outstanding maple syrup and sugar.

Once a customer joked that he would have to take out a bank loan to buy a gallon of syrup. Not quite true! Chuck gave him a crash course in maple syrup production, and the man was stunned to hear that it took forty gallons of sap and countless man-hours to make that one gallon. It would be a bargain at twice the price! When the sap flows, Chuck works day and night boiling it down—he once processed 90,000 gallons in a single session.

And he keeps his sense of humor. To Chuck, fellow producers Tony and Andy Van Glad are known as "the sapheads." Down the market aisle is the flower and plant man, whom he christened "Jack Twig." The family that sells mushrooms, he calls "the Schroom sisters," and the Doxsees, of clam fame, are "the diggers."

MARKET PEOPLE
Bob Doxsee, Jr., and Jack Gunn ("Jack Flash")

Bob Doxsee, Jr., and his daughter, Beth, have been selling clams in Greenmarket since 1987 and are a great source of market lore. Bob is a descendant of J. H. Doxsee, the farmer who started canning Great South Bay hard clams in 1865.

According to Bob Doxsee, "The luckiest guy in the market is Jack Flash," the market nickname of Jack Gunn, a fish and seafood expert who put in many years as a commercial fisherman. One blustery winter day, Jack was serving as mate on the offshore dragger *Tiki* when a fierce storm blew in from the northwest. Jack's skipper ordered the crew to head for home, despite the

Jack Gunn

MAPLE SYRUP TIPS
Howard and Stephan Cantor,
Deep Mountain Maple

Howard Cantor

Maple syrup is graded by color from light to dark, with the darker syrups having more pronounced flavor and hints of caramel. There are four grades, and a well-stocked kitchen should have at least two of them.   Light syrup usually is produced early in the season; as the weather gets warmer, sap gets darker, but the color of the syrup depends upon the skill of the sugar maker. Sap is placed in wide, shallow evaporating pans over very high heat, and the faster it is boiled, the more delicate the results will be.   *Fancy* is light and delicately flavored with hints of vanilla. It is excellent drizzled over ice cream, yogurt, fruit, waffles, French toast, and pancakes.   *Medium Amber* is a shade darker than Fancy, with a more pronounced maple flavor.   *Dark Amber* has a hearty and robust flavor that asserts itself when used in baking. It is not too delicate, yet not too rich and smoky. *Grade B* may also be used at the table, but it is especially good with strong-flavored foods, such as winter squash, sweet potatoes, and roasted meats.   *Buying* You will find maple syrup in metal tins and plastic containers, but do the environmentally sound thing and buy it in reusable glass bottles or jars. Another plus—glass will not impart any flavor to the syrup.   *Storing* Store unopened bottles in a cool, dark place. Once opened, syrup will keep in the refrigerator for up to 6 months.   *Cooking*   Maple syrup can usually be substituted for an equal amount of honey or corn syrup. Similarly, maple sugar can be substituted equally for cane sugar.

fact that it would mean a fourteen-hour trip into the teeth of the wind. As they fought their way back, ice quickly formed on the nets and water rushed up through the rudder shaft box, causing the *Tiki* to start sinking at the stern. It was a fierce winter night, below freezing, and a gale was blowing.

Mercifully, the Coast Guard sent a helicopter, but the ship's rigging was so heavy with ice that the men could not be safely lifted off the deck. When the helicopter became dangerously low on fuel and had to abandon them, they were forced to jump ship and board an inflatable life raft, and try their luck on the stormy sea. Fortunately, they all lived to tell the tale. The last anyone saw of the *Tiki,* she was going under with lights still blazing.

Winter Squash

Grown in Mexico as far back as 9000 B.C., squash was one of the earliest foods cultivated by native Americans, but until recently, pumpkin and acorn have been the two most common varieties. Face it, no one has ever heard Charlie Brown's friend Linus say, "Let's wait for the Great Buttercup Squash to arrive."

Greenmarket's farmers have led the way out of the pumpkin patch into a new era of heirloom and hybrid squash, with thirty varieties gracing their tables. Green acorn has been joined by its golden and white cousins, as well as by Red Kuri, Calabaza, Sweet Dumpling, Banana, and Hokkaido.

WINTER SQUASH TIPS

Buying   Look for smooth skins that have no cuts or soft spots.   *Storing*   Keep squash in a dry, cool place—definitely not in the refrigerator.

Traditionally, a squash is cut in half, cleaned out in the middle, and roasted; but other cooking methods have also become popular. Most varieties of winter squash are scrumptious roasted, steamed, baked, stir-fried, grilled, or broiled. Mix a few types together for extra flavor.

Winter Squash Chart

New York's Greenmarkets are an ethnic crossroads, and their customers reflect the city's diverse cultural mix. In response, many farmers have begun to grow fruit and vegetables that are nontraditional to their farming regions, for example, Calabaza squash, a Caribbean and Central American favorite now very much at home in New York City.

Alex Paffenroth grows some of the most interesting varieties of winter squash seen at Greenmarket. We developed this chart together.

Some of the squash listed below are quite portable, and it's easy to toss two or three into your market basket; but others are too large to carry comfortably. Don't worry, sellers will hack off chunks of Calabaza or Hubbard so that you can enjoy their unique flavor even when you are cooking for only a small group. Of course, if you and several friends are in excellent shape, you're welcome to buy a fifty-pound Pink Banana, lug it home, and serve it to the whole neighborhood.

Winter

Variety and Appearance	Taste and Texture	Let's Eat!
Blue Kuri Offspring of the *Hubbard;* smaller and flatter than the *Red Kuri*. Soft-toned, blue-green skin may be mottled or warted; yellow-orange flesh. Weighs 3 to 5 pounds.	Fine texture and rich taste.	Good cut into chunks and stir-fried or cooked tempura style. Try it in pies.
Buttercup Squat, turban-shaped; dark-green skin on top with a pale-green button on the bottom; occasional warts or blemishes; flesh can be deep-yellow or orange. Weighs 2 to 5 pounds.	Fine texture; exceptionally sweet, delicious, nutty flavor.	Split in half and baked with a little butter, salt, and pepper, *Buttercup* equals squash perfection.
Calabaza Large, round shape; dark-green skin with yellow undertone; rich orange flesh. Weighs 10 pounds.	Fine texture; meaty, sweet flesh.	Best used in soups and stews or cooked on a grill. A favorite in Caribbean and Central American cuisine.
Delicata Tube-shaped; creamy pale-green to orange skin with vertical stripes; orange flesh. Weighs 2 pounds.	Similar in texture and flavor to sweet potatoes.	Excellent roasted with butter and maple syrup; good steamed.
Hubbard Wide in the middle and pulled to a point on each end; the top is often twisted or slightly folded over on itself in the fashion of Sleepy the Dwarf's hat. Dusty, blue-green or orange bumpy skin; pale-yellow flesh. Often weighs over 20 pounds.	Softer texture than other winter squash; mellow, subtle taste.	Makes excellent soup; use the halved shell as a serving bowl. Stuff halves with vegetables, tofu, or tempeh. Perfect for purees and baked goods. *Hubbards* make beautiful table, mantel, and front-porch decorations.
Kabocha Developed in Japan. Flattened globe shape (some varieties are more rounded than flat), ribbed sides. Skin ranges from gray-green to dull brown or orange; deep-orange flesh. Weighs up to 5 pounds.	Dense, dry, flaky flesh; rich sweet flavor has hints of pumpkin and sweet potato.	Excellent braised or in stews. Often served tempura style in Japanese restaurants.

Farmer Alex Paffenroth and Joel Patraker's Winter Squash Adviser

Variety and Appearance	Taste and Texture	Let's Eat!
Lakota Large bright-orange teardrop shape with patches of dark green; orange-yellow flesh. Hard to find except in farmers' markets. Weighs 5 to 7 pounds.	Fine-grained texture; good balance of sweet and nutty flavors.	Excellent choice for baking and pies.
Long Island Cheese Pumpkin Popular older variety that, like the larger, less tasty *Cheese Pumpkin*, got its name because of a resemblance to the standard cheesebox of the early 1800s. Smooth tan skin and slightly ribbed, flattened shape; deep-orange flesh. Weighs 6 to 10 pounds.	Coarse texture; sweet flesh.	Excellent in pies, muffins, ice cream.
Orange Hokkaido (also known as **Red Kuri**) A cousin of the *Hubbard,* with an elongated pearlike shape; smooth electric-reddish-orange skin, bright-red flesh. Weighs 4 to 10 pounds.	Thick, fine-grained texture; sweet, strong, nutty flavor.	Use in pies, bread pudding, and risotto; good steamed.
Pink Banana Tube-shaped, 4 feet long; bright-pink skin; pastel-orange flesh. Can weigh more than 50 pounds (it halts customers in their tracks).	Fine texture and sweet taste.	Best baked or in pies; good for purees.

Potatoes
Joel Patraker: Potato Detective

Rex and Susan Mongold—remember those names! This California couple has changed the eating habits of New Yorkers.

In the late 1980s, Tony Mannetta (then Greenmarket's assistant director) and I visited California and had the pleasure of meeting the Mongolds at a farming conference. On their farm in the foothills of the Sierra Nevada Mountains, they cultivate twenty unusual varieties of potatoes—not an Idaho or a Russet among them, but plenty of Caribes, Ruby Crescents, Cherries Jubilee, Peanuts, Carole Rose Firs, and the Mel Brooks of spuds, Purple Peruvian Fingerlings (a venerable potato grown in South America for at least 2,000 years). Their diverse shapes, sizes, and colors and their variety of rich flavors have brought about a revolution in potato cuisine.

Meeting the Mongolds and their potatoes, I felt as if I had discovered a new world. I returned to New York with three extra suitcases filled with seed potatoes and set about trying to convince farmer friends that they should start growing these special varieties. But my enthusiasm seemed not to be contagious, and few showed more than a passing interest.

I have always believed that you must open your umbrella and honor the rain, if you want the sun to shine, so I was patient. And sure enough, just when I came close to admitting defeat, a farmer named Rick Bishop pulled me aside at Greenmarket and bought the potatoes!

Today, Rick grows about twenty varieties of potatoes on his Mountain Sweet Berry Farm. He had

POTATO TIPS

Buying   Avoid tubers that have any soft spots or bruises.   If the skin has a green tip or overall hue, the potato has been exposed to too much light and will give the eater a severe stomachache. The green-tipped potatoes may be used safely once the colored areas have been cut off, but avoid the ones that have overall green coloring.   *Storing*   Store potatoes in any dark, dry, cool place. They don't need to be refrigerated.

been up to sixty-four, but a 1994 potato blight—like the infamous one in Ireland—hit him hard, reducing him to twelve varieties. He has been steadily building up his stock ever since. "Some people collect antiques—I collect potatoes," he says, but he has a larger goal. "I want to keep alive the wild potatoes of the world and to make this rich heritage available to everyone."

Potato Chart

Potatoes, like most other vegetables available at Greenmarket, come in a variety of shapes and sizes. They can be narrow and oblong, like the Carola, or egg-shaped, like the Charlotte. New Reds look like marbles or golf balls; Peanuts may remind you of large, plump teardrops; and when you see the Russian Banana, you will agree that it got its name for a good reason. Fingerlings (such as La Ratte, Purple Peruvian, and Ruby Crescent) resemble the shape of a human finger, and are one to eight inches long—that's not small potatoes.

Variety and Appearance	Texture and Taste	Let's Eat!
Caribe Magenta skin, creamy, snow-white flesh; can weigh more than $\frac{1}{2}$ pound each.	Creamy texture; robust flavor, richest tasting of white varieties.	Excellent mashed, baked, or as homefries.
Carola Smooth, shiny, golden-yellow skin; firm, light-yellow flesh. Medium-size, narrow, and somewhat oblong.	Moist and creamy with delicate, buttery flavor.	Bake, boil, roast, or fry, but no butter please! Keep it simple.
Charlotte Dull yellow skin, yellow flesh; oblong shape. This French favorite looks like an egg.	Somewhat starchy, very dense and moist, with earthy flavor.	All purpose: potato salads, mashed, steamed, roasted.
La Ratte A fingerling grown in France since the late 1800s. Small to medium, with a thin, pale-yellow skin, yellow flesh.	Waxy, smooth texture; rich flavor with overtones of chestnut and almond.	Mash it up! Add a little nutmeg, or olive oil blended with a few fresh basil leaves.
New Red Pinkish-red, papery skin, creamy-white flesh; marble to golf-ball size.	Waxy flesh; mild taste.	Excellent in potato salads, or with chopped fresh herbs and olive oil.
Ozette Indian A long (up to 8 inches) odd-shaped fingerling with smooth, creamy-white skin and yellowish flesh. In the late 1700s, Spanish adventurers brought it from Peru to what is now Washington State's Olympic Peninsula and traded it with the region's Ozette Indians.	Creamy texture; excellent flavor with a hint of nuts.	Good for steaming and boiling. Slice the larger ones into $\frac{1}{2}$-inch disks and roast.
Papa Amarilla One of the fathers of all potatoes, originating in the Peruvian Andes—the cradle of potato civilization. Odd looking and lumpy; yellow skin with hints of purple; the brightest yellow flesh of any potato.	Fine-grained, dry texture; hearty flavor.	Perfect for baking or boiling. In Peru, children love its inviting taste.

Winter

Variety and Appearance	Texture and Taste	Let's Eat!
Peanut Teardrop-shaped, fat fingerling with buff or light-tan skin; deep-yellow flesh.	Dense texture; big, nutty flavor.	Holds its shape well when cooked; a good choice for salads and roasting.
Purple Peruvian A knobby fingerling covered with a papery, dusty-purple skin; amazing deep-violet flesh.	Dry texture with a rich, earthy taste.	Treat your family to Hash Purples for breakfast; add an exciting tint to your favorite chowder.
Ruby Crescent A smooth, large fingerling with pinkish-tan skin and yellow flesh.	Moist, dense, and creamy; nutty flavor.	Holds its shape when cooked; try it in soups, potato salads, or stews.
Russian Banana Medium-size, banana-shaped fingerling; yellow skin, pale-yellow flesh.	Waxy texture, earthy taste.	Remains firm when boiled. Good in salads.

David and Hong-An at the Oak Grove Plantation stand with Farmer Ted Blew and his son, Eric

EILEEN DASPIN AND CESARE CASELLA

Pickled Shallots (Scalogno Sott'olio)

Eileen Daspin is a Greenmarket customer who writes for The Wall Street Journal. *Cesare Casella often walks around with a big bouquet of herbs stuffed in his jacket pocket, so if you met him you'd think he had just stepped out of the garden outside his family's restaurant in Tuscany.*

The hardest part of this recipe is putting the shallots aside in the kitchen and not tasting them until they are pickled and ready to enjoy. The shallots will make a beautiful addition to a relish tray along with pickles, olives, celery, and carrots.

Makes 1 quart

3	quarts water
1	quart large shallots (about 1½ pounds), peeled
2	teaspoons salt
2½	quarts white vinegar
1½	pints olive oil, or enough to cover the shallots
6	basil leaves
	Pinch of red pepper flakes
	Whole cloves (about 3)

In a large pot, bring the water to a boil and add the shallots. Add the salt and 2 tablespoons of the vinegar. Let the shallots boil for 2 minutes, then drain and cool. Place in a large jar, cover with the remaining vinegar, and put the lid on the jar. Let sit in a cool place for 3 days.

Drain the shallots and pour in olive oil to cover. Stir in the basil, red pepper flakes, and cloves, making sure they are well distributed. Allow to sit for 2 days in a cool place. Check the shallots to make sure they are covered with oil. If necessary, add more oil.

Leave the shallots on a shelf, out of direct light, in a cool, dark place. They will be ready to eat in 2 months.

EILEEN DASPIN AND CESARE CASELLA
Bread and Cabbage Soup
(Minestra di Pane e Verze)

As you move from fall into winter, or in the early days of winter when the market still has a nice selection, this hearty Tuscan soup from my friends Eileen and Cesare will warm you inside and out.

1	tablespoon olive oil
1	medium carrot, diced
1	stalk celery, diced
1½	medium onions, finely chopped
3	cloves garlic, thinly sliced
2	scallions, thinly sliced
1	rosemary sprig, leaves only, coarsey chopped (1 teaspoon)
6	sage leaves, coarsely chopped (scant tablespoon)
¼	teaspoon red pepper flakes
¾	cup white wine
2	medium white potatoes, chopped into ½-inch dice
½	of a 2-pound head Savoy cabbage, cored and cut into ¾-inch dice
3	cups water or vegetable stock
2	cups cooked or canned red kidney, pinto, or cannellini beans (one 15- to 19-ounce can, drained and rinsed)
½	cup peeled and crushed canned Italian tomatoes
½	to 1 teaspoon salt
	Freshly ground pepper
4	slices crusty bread, Tuscan if possible
1	or 2 garlic cloves, halved

Makes 4 to 6 servings
(2 quarts)

In a Dutch oven over medium-low heat, warm the olive oil. Add the carrot, celery, onions, garlic, scallions, rosemary, sage, and red pepper flakes and cook, stirring occasionally, until soft, about 10 minutes. Raise the heat to medium, add the wine, and bring to a simmer. Add the potatoes, cabbage, and water, cover, and simmer for 30 minutes. If the soup is too thick, add a little water.

Stir in the beans, tomatoes, salt, and pepper, and simmer 30 minutes, uncovered, stirring frequently and adding water as necessary. (Add water during the last 20 minutes of cooking only if you want a thinner soup.)

Toast the bread slices and rub both sides with a cut garlic clove. Place each slice in the bottom of a wide, shallow soup dish, ladle in the soup, and serve.

TRUDY AND STANLEY OSCZEPINSKI
Italian Sweet Red Onion Salad

The S and SO stand has been with us since the first market opened on West Fifty-ninth Street in 1976. "Stosh" Osczepinski and his family, who run it, are farmers in the Pine Island region of New York State, and this onion salad is one of the things they make at home in the winter. It is so basic: just get some red onions, vinegar, water, sugar, salt, and pepper, and there you go.

2	pounds red onions, peeled, halved, and sliced thinly
1	cup olive oil
1$^1/_2$	cups red wine vinegar
$^3/_4$	cup sugar
$^1/_2$	teaspoon salt
$^1/_8$	teaspoon freshly ground pepper

Makes 4 cups

Place the onions in a large bowl. In a separate bowl, combine the olive oil, vinegar, sugar, salt, and pepper and pour over the onions. Cover and let stand at room temperature for about 2 hours; then refrigerate up to 2 days.

PETER IVY

Fingerling Potato and Arugula Salad

Chef Peter Ivy gives us this very simple potato salad in the French style, dressed with a vinaigrette. Use your favorite flavorful fingerlings.

$1^1/_2$	pounds fingerling potatoes (about 20), washed
$1/_3$	cup olive oil
8	garlic cloves, thinly sliced
2	tablespoons raspberry vinegar or red wine vinegar
2	bunches of arugula, washed and dried
$1/_2$	teaspoon salt
$1/_4$	teaspoon freshly ground pepper

Makes 4 to 6 servings

Place the potatoes in a large saucepan and cover with cold salted water. Bring to a boil. Reduce the heat and simmer until tender, about 20 minutes. Drain and let cool to room temperature. Slice crosswise $1/_2$ inch thick.

Meanwhile, in a medium skillet, heat the olive oil over medium heat. Add the garlic and cook, stirring, until it starts to color, about 3 minutes. Stir in the vinegar. Set aside to cool.

Place the arugula in a large bowl, pour the cooled dressing over it, and mix well. Add the potato slices and mix well. Season with salt and pepper.

LORELEI JOY BORLAND

Market Mushroom Risotto

Risottos are something new to me—my wife and I have only recently started to cook them at home. We were pleasantly surprised at the simplicity of Lorelei's recipe, which provides a great vehicle for the rich variety of mushrooms available at Greenmarket.

6	tablespoons butter
1	pound mixed mushrooms, such as portobello, stemmed, trimmed, and thinly sliced; shiitake, stemmed and sliced $1/4$ inch thick; and cremini, thinly sliced
$5^1/2$	cups chicken stock or mushroom broth
3	tablespoons olive oil
1	small onion, minced
1	large garlic clove, preferably Rocambole, minced
$1^1/2$	cups Arborio rice (about 8 ounces)
$1/2$	cup finely chopped Italian parsley
$1/4$	cup grated Parmesan cheese, plus extra for the table
$1/2$	teaspoon salt
	Freshly ground pepper

Makes 4 servings

Melt 3 tablespoons of the butter in a large heavy saucepan over medium-high heat. Add the mushrooms and cook until wilted, about 5 minutes. Transfer the mushrooms to a bowl and set aside.

Meanwhile, in a medium saucepan over medium-low heat, bring the stock barely to a simmer. Keep over very low heat while continuing the risotto.

Over low heat, warm the oil in the saucepan used for the mushrooms. Add the onion and cook until softened, about 5 minutes. Add the garlic and cook 1 minute more. Add the rice and stir for 1 minute.

Raise the heat to medium, add about $1/2$ cup of stock, and stir constantly until the mixture comes to a gentle simmer. Slowly add the remaining stock, $1/2$ cup at a time, stirring constantly until each addition is absorbed and the rice is al dente and creamy, about 18 minutes total.

Stir in the mushrooms, the remaining 3 tablespoons butter, the parsley, Parmesan, and salt.

Serve at once with freshly ground pepper to taste and more Parmesan.

KEVIN JOHNSON

Grange Hall Beet and Potato Latkes

I was delighted when Chef Kevin Johnson and owner Jay Savulich of Grange Hall restaurant offered me this recipe, because in my Jewish heritage, potato latkes are an important part of the Chanukah celebration. This version updates the traditional pancakes with the addition of another root vegetable, sweet red beets. In my house, latkes were garnished with sour cream, but Kevin offers you the lighter alternative of yogurt. Either can be combined with fresh dill, but if the dill isn't fresh, you don't want to use it!

1	large (8-ounce) baking potato (such as Caribe), peeled and coarsely grated
2	medium (4 ounces) red beets, peeled and coarsely grated
1	small yellow onion, coarsely grated
1	large egg, lightly beaten
$1/4$	cup flour
$3/4$	teaspoon salt
	Freshly ground black pepper to taste
$1/3$	cup canola oil
$1/4$	cup sour cream or yogurt, for garnish
2	tablespoons minced fresh dill, for garnish (do *not* use dried dill)

Makes twelve 3-inch pancakes, serving 4 as a first course or side dish

Rinse the grated potatoes in a bowl of cold water. Remove the potato shreds with your fingers to a clean kitchen towel. Roll up in the towel and squeeze dry.

Place the beets and onions in a large colander and strongly squeeze out the excess moisture.

In a bowl, stir together the potato, beets, onion, eggs, flour, salt, and pepper to taste.

Heat $1/4$ cup of the canola oil in a cast-iron skillet over medium-high heat. Add 4 heaping tablespoons of batter to the pan to form 4 pancakes; flatten slightly. Cook about 5 minutes, turning once, until golden brown on both sides. Keep warm on a rack set over a baking sheet in a low oven. Repeat with the remaining potato mixture and $1\frac{1}{3}$ tablespoons of oil.

Top each pancake with a teaspoon of sour cream or yogurt and sprinkle with fresh dill. Serve at once.

BILL TELEPAN
Herbed Spaetzle

Chef Bill Telepan serves these light dumplings alongside his Roasted Pork Loin with a Walnut-Savory Crust (see page 156).

2   eggs, at room temperature
1   egg yolk, at room temperature
$\frac{1}{3}$ cup milk, slightly warmed
2   tablespoons unsalted butter, softened
3   tablespoons coarsely chopped Italian parsley or mixed fresh herbs
1   teaspoon salt
$\frac{1}{4}$ teaspoon freshly ground pepper
1   cup flour
    Olive oil for drizzling

Makes 8 side-dish servings

Bring a large saucepan of lightly salted water to a boil.

Meanwhile, in a small bowl, whisk together the eggs, egg yolk, milk, butter, parsley, salt, and pepper. Add the flour and stir until incorporated. The batter will be loose and elastic.

Press the mixture through a colander or ricer into the boiling water; the spaetzle will rise to the top when cooked.

Drain and cool under cold running water. Drain and drizzle with a little olive oil, to prevent sticking. Makes 3 cups. Can be reheated in a skillet with a little oil or butter.

EDWIN A. YOWELL

Mushroom, Ham, and Goat Cheese Frittata

This full-flavored Italian-style omelette comes from Ed Yowell, an enthusiastic Greenmarket customer, who creates imaginative market-based recipes. There's nothing better than a frittata for a weekend brunch or early dinner, especially this one, made with tempting market ingredients.

2	tablespoons butter
1	medium yellow onion, cut into $1/3$-inch dice
$1/3$	pound shiitake mushrooms, stemmed and cut into $1/2$-inch dice
$1/3$	pound cremini mushrooms, quartered
	About $1/4$ cup dry red wine
1	large russet potato, boiled or baked, peeled, and cut into $1/2$-inch dice
$1/4$	pound piece smoked ham cut into $1/4$-inch dice (about $2/3$ cup)
$1/4$	teaspoon freshly ground white or black pepper
$1/2$	teaspoon fresh thyme leaves
	Pinch salt
5	large eggs, well beaten
3	ounces fresh goat cheese, crumbled (scant cup)

Makes 4 servings

Preheat the broiler.

In a large ovenproof skillet over medium-high heat, melt the butter. Add the onion and cook until lightly caramelized, about 5 minutes. Add the mushrooms and cook, stirring often, until the mushrooms are browned and soft, about 5 minutes. Add the red wine and cook, stirring, until nearly dry, about 5 minutes.

Stir in the potato, ham, pepper, thyme, and salt. Reduce the heat to low and pour the eggs on top, swirling to cover the onion mixture. Cover and cook until the eggs are solid underneath, about 5 minutes. Uncover and place the pan under the broiler until the top is lightly golden. Sprinkle with the goat cheese and return to the broiler until the cheese is soft, about 1 minute.

BRENDAN WALSH
Buttercup Squash Spoonbread

Chef Brendan Walsh of The Elms Restaurant in Connecticut was one of the earliest New York chefs to advocate seasonal cooking and the use of local ingredients. He even invited me to his restaurant kitchen to give a lecture on garlic and explain the differences between the locally grown and imported bulbs. I know at least a dozen chefs who came out of his famous southwestern-style restaurant, Arizona 206, and who keep his training as the essence of their cooking.

This vegetable-rich spoonbread, made with Greenmarket ingredients, can be baked ahead of time and rewarmed. Serve it alongside roasted meat or game, or as a main course accompanied by steamed greens or grilled leeks.

2	pounds buttercup squash, about 2 squash, halved
	Butter for greasing the baking dish
4	cups whole milk
1	cup heavy cream
4	large eggs, separated
1/4	cup honey
1	teaspoon baking powder
1	tablespoon salt
1/8	teaspoon ground cloves, or substitute nutmeg
4	tablespoons (1/2 stick) unsalted butter, plus melted butter for drizzling
2	cups coarse yellow cornmeal

Makes 10 servings

Preheat the oven to 400°F. Place the squash halves on a baking sheet cut side down. Bake until tender when pierced with a fork, about 1 hour. When cool enough to handle, scoop out the seeds and discard, and mash or puree the flesh. You should have about 2 cups.

Reduce the oven to 375°F. Butter a 2½-quart shallow baking dish.

In a large bowl, whisk together the squash puree, milk, cream, egg yolks, honey, baking powder, salt, and cloves. Whisk in the butter, then the cornmeal. Set aside.

In a separate bowl, beat the egg whites with an electric mixer until stiff but not dry. Fold ⅓ of the whites into the squash mixture. Fold in the remaining whites. Scrape into the prepared baking dish.

Bake in the center of the oven until set around the outside and wobbly in the center, 25 to 30 minutes. Let cool 10 minutes, then serve.

JEFF RENKEL
Root Vegetable Gratin

Jeff is one of the talented young chefs you meet at the market who have worked at some of the finest New York kitchens. His sweet combination of root vegetables takes the classic potato gratin to new heights. You can layer the vegetables as you prefer, but we like this order: parsnip, potato, sweet potato, celery root.

2   cups heavy cream
1   cup whole milk
1   bay leaf
2   sprigs thyme
6   leaves sage
    Pinch of grated nutmeg (optional)
2   teaspoons kosher salt
    Butter for greasing a casserole
3   parsnips (1/2 pound)
3   Idaho potatoes (1 1/2 pounds)
1   sweet potato (3/4 pound)
1   small celery root (3/4 pound)
1/2   Spanish onion, finely chopped
1/4   cup all-purpose flour
    Freshly ground pepper

Makes 4 servings

Place the cream and milk in a medium saucepan with the bay leaf, thyme, sage, nutmeg, and salt and bring to a simmer over medium heat. Take off the heat and let steep for 1/2 hour, then strain (may be refrigerated up to 1 day).

Preheat the oven to 350°F. Butter a 2 1/2-quart shallow casserole or gratin.

Meanwhile, peel the parsnips, potatoes, sweet potato, and celery root and place in a bowl of cold water. Slice the vegetables thinly using a mandoline or similar slicer. Alternate layers of sliced root vegetables with the onion, flour, and cream mixure in the casserole, seasoning each layer with pepper. Adjust the amount of cream, if necessary, so that the vegetables are just standing in the cream.

Cover snugly with foil. Bake 45 minutes, uncover, and bake 15 minutes more, until golden. Let rest 30 minutes before serving.

BILL TELEPAN
Braised Winter Greens

The deep, earthy flavors of winter greens come through with gentle braising, and the vegetables are tender and silky. Serve these greens with Chef Telepan's Roasted Pork Loin with a Walnut-Savory Crust (see page 156).

1/4   cup (1/2 stick) unsalted butter
1   onion, finely chopped
2   pounds braising greens, such as chard, mustard, escarole,
      or turnip tops, coarsely chopped, washed, and lightly drained
1/2   teaspoon salt
1/4   teaspoon freshly ground pepper

Makes 8 servings

Melt the butter in a deep skillet over medium heat. Add the onion and cook, stirring, until soft, about 6 minutes. Add the greens with any water clinging to the leaves and cook until tender, about 15 minutes. Season with the salt and pepper.

BILL TELEPAN
Roasted Squash Puree

Chef Bill Telepan roasts the squash to bring out its deeper flavors. This dish is appropriate for fall, as well as winter. Serve it alongside his Roasted Pork Loin with a Walnut-Savory Crust (see page 156).

I also like this as a spread on fresh market bread.

4   pounds squash (delicata or buttercup), halved and seeded
12   tablespoons butter
      Salt and freshly ground pepper

Makes 8 servings

Preheat the oven to 400°F.

Place the squash in a roasting pan, rub with 4 tablespoons of the butter, and season with salt and pepper. Pour about 1/2 cup of water into the pan, cover with foil, and roast until the squash is tender, about 1 hour.

Scoop out the squash flesh into a strainer and let sit, weighted down, until fairly dry. Mix with the remaining butter, taste and season, and keep warm.

Sweet and Sour Red Cabbage (Rotkraut)

Tom's passion has been to track the history and the lives of people who entered the United States through Ellis Island. His Ellis Island Immigrant Cookbook, *from which this recipe is borrowed, tells what brought them to this country and shares some of their culinary gifts. This recipe was given to Tom Bernardin by Kristine Kindel of Greendale, Wisconsin, who arrived from Austria on May 27, 1927.*

Although the original recipe doesn't suggest it, try crumbling the crisp bacon strips over the cooked cabbage. Delicious!

1	head red cabbage (2 pounds), cored and shredded
2	tablespoons bacon drippings (from 2 strips bacon)
1	small onion, finely chopped
1/2	cup red wine vinegar
3	medium apples, peeled, cored, and cut in 1/2-inch dice
1/2	cup light brown sugar
3/4	teaspoon salt
1/4	teaspoon freshly ground pepper
2	tablespoons cornstarch
1 1/2	cups water

Makes 4 servings

Put the shredded cabbage in a colander, pour 2 quarts of boiling water over it, and let drain.

Heat the bacon drippings in a large skillet over medium heat and cook the onion until transparent, about 7 minutes. Add the cabbage, vinegar, apples, brown sugar, salt, and pepper and simmer 30 minutes.

In a small bowl, stir together the cornstarch and the water, then stir into the red cabbage. Simmer 5 minutes longer, until no longer cloudy.

Baked Jerusalem Artichoke Chips

A Greenmarket customer turned chef, and graduate of the French Culinary Institute, Ilene can be seen daily with her yellow scarf tied pirate-style around her forehead, shopping in the market. She offers us this simple recipe for a common but often overlooked root crop. The chips are light and tasty.

1	pound Jerusalem artichokes, unpeeled and scrubbed well
1/4	cup canola oil
1/2	teaspoon kosher salt, plus extra if desired
	Freshly ground pepper

Makes 4 servings

Preheat the oven to 400°F.

With a large, sharp knife, box grater, or mandoline, slice the chokes lengthwise 1/8 inch thick. In a large bowl, toss the slices with oil to coat. Arrange in a single layer on a large baking sheet; do not crowd. Sprinkle with salt and pepper. Bake until golden brown, about 12 minutes, rotating the pan occasionally for even cooking.

Remove from the oven and sprinkle with additional salt, if desired. Let cool before removing from the pan with a metal spatula.

RICK BISHOP
Hash Brown Purples

Rick Bishop grows Peruvian Purple Fingerling Potatoes, as well as many other unusual potato varieties, on his farm in the Catskills (see Rick's Potato Chart, page 137).

This is a modern version of a traditional breakfast side dish, using a very old variety of potato. Rick recommends serving these savory potatoes with fresh eggs from Greenmarket.

A tip on flipping: be sure to wear oven mitts!

1	pound purple fingerling potatoes, scrubbed but not peeled
1/4	teaspoon salt
1/4	teaspoon freshly ground black pepper
1 1/2	tablespoons vegetable oil
1 1/2	tablespoons butter

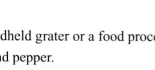

Makes 4 servings

Grate the potatoes, using the large holes of a handheld grater or a food processor with a medium grating disk. Toss with the salt and pepper.

Heat the oil and butter in a 9-inch cast-iron skillet over medium heat. Add the shredded potatoes to the pan, pressing to make an even cake. Cover and cook for 10 minutes. Use a spatula to loosen the bottom, invert a plate on top, flip, then slide the cake back into the pan. Cook uncovered for 10 minutes longer. Cut into wedges and serve hot.

RUSSIAN BANANA
fingerling potatoes
thin skinned $2.50/ lb.
yellow fleshed
BOIL or ROAST

Rick Bishop

JIM GRILLO

The Grouchy Gourmet's Coq au Vin

Here is the aromatic dish that Jim Grillo, "the grouchy gourmet," cooks at his market stand to attract customers on cold winter days, using his fresh Northshire Farm's chickens. If you've been fortunate enough to gather round the simmering stew, you will surely want to duplicate his sorcery at home.

2	small (about 3 pounds each) broiler chickens, each cut into eighths
	Salt and freshly ground pepper
1	tablespoon olive oil
3	large garlic cloves, smashed
3	large red onions, halved and sliced $1/4$ inch thick (2 pounds)
1	bottle (750 ml) hearty red wine, such as Burgundy, Cabernet Sauvignon, or Chianti
4	cups water or chicken stock
	Dried basil, or fresh, if available, optional
	Dried oregano, or fresh, if available, optional
4	tablespoons unsalted butter
1	pound white button mushrooms, quartered
3	tablespoons flour

Makes 8 servings

Season the chickens with $1/2$ teaspoon salt and $1/4$ teaspoon pepper. Heat 1 tablespoon oil in a large Dutch oven over medium-high heat. Add half of the chicken pieces and cook until nicely browned, about 12 minutes. Transfer with tongs to a plate and repeat with the remaining chicken.

Add the garlic and onions to the pot, cover, and cook, stirring occasionally, over medium heat until softened, about 10 minutes.

Return the chicken to the pot. Pour in the wine and water, and add the dried basil and oregano, if using. Bring to a boil partially covered. Reduce the heat and simmer gently, skimming as necessary, until the chicken is very tender, about 1 hour.

Melt 1 tablespoon of the butter in a large skillet over medium heat. Add the mushrooms and cook, stirring occasionally, until nicely browned. Stir into the stew. Season to taste with salt and pepper. Add the fresh basil and oregano, if using.

With a fork, mix the remaining 3 tablespoons butter with the flour to make a paste. Whisk into the stew. Simmer for 5 minutes longer, until slightly thickened. (This can be prepared up to 2 days ahead, but add the fresh herbs shortly before serving.) Let cool completely, then cover and refrigerate. Rewarm over medium heat, stirring gently.

JOYCE QUATTROCIOCCHI

Roast Pheasant with Wild Rice and Pheasant Sausage Stuffing

The Quattrociocchi family of Quattro's Game Farm has been farming since before World War II and bringing their excellent free-range pheasants and turkeys to New Yorkers for years. They make a sensational pheasant sausage—everybody who tastes it at their Greenmarket stand becomes a customer. This family recipe shows a good way to use wild rice, and an easy method for roasting pheasant.

Make sure the stuffing is cool or cold before stuffing the pheasant. Never stuff a bird with hot stuffing!

**FOR THE STUFFING
(PREPARE UP TO A DAY AHEAD)**

1	cup wild rice
2½	cups water
1	bay leaf
	Salt and freshly ground pepper
¼	cup olive oil
1	pound fresh pheasant sausage, casings removed
1	onion, minced
1	stalk celery, finely chopped
2	garlic cloves, peeled and smashed
1	pound button mushrooms, cleaned, stemmed, and thinly sliced

Makes 4 servings

Combine the rice, water, bay leaf, and salt and pepper to taste in a medium pot and bring to a boil. Reduce the heat, cover, and simmer until the rice is popped and tender, about 45 minutes. Remove the bay leaf.

Meanwhile, heat the oil in a large skillet over medium heat. Add the sausage and cook, breaking up the meat with a wooden spoon, until browned, about 7 minutes. Transfer the sausage with a slotted spoon to a large bowl, and set aside.

Add the onion and celery to the pan and cook, stirring, until translucent; add the garlic and cook 1 minute. Add the mushrooms and cook until golden, about 5 minutes. Add this mixture to the cooked rice and sausage, mix well, and let cool completely. Cover and refrigerate overnight, if desired.

FOR THE PHEASANT BROTH

Neck and giblets from two 3-pound pheasants
1½ cups water
½ leek, cleaned
½ carrot, peeled and cut in 2 pieces
½ onion, peeled and cut in 2 pieces
Salt and freshly ground pepper

Combine all ingredients in a saucepan over medium heat and simmer 30 to 45 minutes. Strain.

FOR THE PHEASANT

Two 3-pound pheasants, giblets and neck removed, rinsed
1 garlic clove, smashed
3 tablespoons olive oil to coat the birds
1 large onion, thinly sliced
2 cups pheasant broth (or chicken or vegetable broth)
½ teaspoon salt
¼ teaspoon freshly ground pepper

Preheat the oven to 450°F. Rub the pheasants outside and inside with the garlic and the olive oil, stuff loosely with the cooled stuffing, and truss securely with pins or string.

Scatter the sliced onion on the bottom of a large roasting pan and place the pheasants on top, breast side down. Pour the broth over the birds and season with the salt and pepper. Roast for 15 minutes, turn breast side up, and roast another 20 minutes (the breasts should be nice and brown). Reduce the heat to 350°F, baste with pan juices, and cover with foil. Roast, basting occasionally, until the juices run clear or the drumsticks wiggle loosely, another 1½ to 2 hours.

Carve and serve with the stuffing and pan juices.

BILL TELEPAN

Roasted Pork Loin with a Walnut-Savory Crust

Chef Bill Telepan of JUdson Grill is a master of hearty dishes, although he is thin as a rail. This dish, highlighting fresh pork from Greenmarket with walnuts and piquant winter savory, will sustain you through winter.

The chef suggests serving this with his rich version of a squash puree, braised winter greens, and herbed spaetzle. (See the recipes in this chapter.)

1	boneless pork loin, about 3 pounds
1/4	teaspoon salt
1/4	teaspoon freshly ground pepper
2	heads garlic, halved crosswise
1	tablespoon olive oil
1	cup shelled walnuts
1/2	cup fresh white breadcrumbs
3	tablespoons Italian parsley leaves
2	tablespoons winter savory leaves

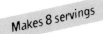

Makes 8 servings

Preheat the oven to 400°F.

Season the pork loin with salt and pepper, place on a rack in a roasting pan, and roast to an internal temperature of 140°F, about 45 minutes. Remove from the oven, cover loosely with foil, and let stand for 15 minutes.

While the pork is roasting, place the garlic in a small baking pan, drizzle with the olive oil, season with salt and pepper, and roast in the oven with the pork until soft, 20 to 30 minutes. When cool, separate the cloves and squeeze out the garlic puree. Set aside.

Place the walnuts in a baking pan and roast in the hot oven until lightly toasted, about 7 minutes. Let cool, then place the nuts, breadcrumbs, and herbs in a food processor and pulse until finely chopped. Reserve.

Smear one side of the pork loin with the roasted garlic and cover with the walnut-breadcrumb mixture. Place in the hot oven until lightly browned, 8 to 10 minutes. Carve into ½-inch-thick slices and place on a serving platter.

ARTHUR SCHWARTZ

Turkey Sausage with Apples and Onions

Arthur Schwartz, the well-known radio food-and-dining personality, is also a successful cookbook author. He tells us: "Apples and onions may seem like an odd combination, but it's an old New England pairing. When you go to Greenmarket in February, you see that apples and onions, potatoes, turnips, and beets—the produce traditionally put down in the cellar for storage during the winter—are about the only fresh produce you can count on. Of course, there are also cheese, baked goods, fresh-pressed cider, farm-made preserves, and at my market at the Grand Army Plaza in Brooklyn, Di Paola Farm's turkeys and turkey products, like the delicious turkey sausage that apples and onions accompany so well."

2 pounds turkey sausage
3 tablespoons unsalted butter
2 medium onions, cut lengthwise in $^3/_4$-inch wedges
2 Mutsu apples, peeled, cored, and cut into 1-inch chunks
$^1/_2$ cup water
Freshly ground pepper

Makes 4 servings

Arthur Schwartz

Cut the sausage into 3 to 4-inch lengths and place in a 10-inch skillet or sauté pan with enough water to come about $^1/_3$ inch up the sides of the sausage. Place over medium heat and cook, turning occasionally, until the water has evaporated, about 15 minutes. Add 1 tablespoon butter and continue to cook until the sausage is lightly browned, about 8 minutes. Transfer the sausage to a platter and cover to keep warm.

Add the remaining butter to the skillet and place over medium heat. Add the onions and cook, stirring, until slightly wilted, about 4 minutes. Add the apples and water to the onions and sauté, tossing the apples and onions and scraping the brown bits from the pan. After the water has evaporated, cook until both the apples and onions are lightly browned and the apple chunks are just tender, about 3 minutes.

Spoon the apples and onions over the sausage and serve warm.

JIM GRILLO

Rabbit Sausage-Three Potato Stew

A lot of Jim Grillo's recipes are developed right at the market, where he cooks them in a wok to the delight of passersby. (And despite his nickname, "the grouchy gourmet," he's friendly and pleasant as he cooks.) Jim makes this during the winter, using ingredients he finds at neighboring farmers' stands. If you cook it during summer or fall, substitute fresh basil for the dried. The rabbit sausage is Jim's own, and can't be beat.

1	tablespoon olive oil (or rendered bacon fat)
1	pound fresh rabbit sausage (Northshire Farm's, or any high-quality fresh sausage)
2	large onions, diced
1	head garlic, cloves separated and peeled
2	cups dry white wine
1	teaspoon dried basil (or fresh, if available)
2	pounds potatoes (2 large of 3 different varieties, such as La Ratte, New Red, or Ruby Crescent), halved and sliced $1/4$ inch thick, unpeeled
2	cups (10 ounces) thickly sliced cremini or large white mushrooms
1	quart vegetable stock or chicken stock, or 2 cups stock and 2 cups water Salt and freshly ground pepper
$1/2$	pound goat feta cheese (such as Little Rainbow), crumbled
$1/3$	cup chopped Italian parsley
1	loaf sourdough bread, sliced, for serving

Makes 4 servings

Heat the oil in a 4-quart Dutch oven over medium heat. Add the sausage and cook until nicely browned, about 10 minutes. Transfer with tongs to a board and cut into $1/4$-inch-thick slices. Reserve.

Add the onions to the drippings in the pot and cook, stirring often, until softened, about 6 minutes. Add the garlic and cook 3 minutes. Pour in the wine, add the dried basil, and scrape up any brown bits from the bottom of the pot. Bring to a boil.

Add the potatoes, mushrooms, and stock. Gently stir in the sliced sausage. Cover partially and simmer gently until the potatoes are tender, about 45 minutes. Add the fresh basil, if using.

Season with salt and pepper to taste. Ladle into wide bowls and sprinkle with the cheese and parsley. (This can be refrigerated up to 2 days.) Serve with the bread.

ILENE ROSEN

Maple Butter-Baked Bosc Pear Slices

Chef Ilene Rosen of the City Bakery does things beautifully and simply with just a few ingredients, and in this recipe, she highlights the fresh fall tastes of ripe pears and maple syrup. Black pepper provides a surprising contrast that brings out the sweet flavors. I find these pears delicious served with ice cream.

1/4   cup unsalted butter
3   tablespoons maple syrup
4   large Bosc pears, stems on
    Freshly ground black pepper

Makes 6 servings

Preheat the oven to 400°F.

Melt the butter in a small saucepan over medium-low heat. Cook until the butter browns, about 2 minutes. Pour into a large bowl and stir in the maple syrup. Mix well.

Cut the pears lengthwise into 3/8- to 1/4-inch slices and toss them with the butter mixture to coat. Arrange in a single layer on a sheet pan and sprinkle with pepper to taste. Bake, turning several times for even cooking, until caramelized to a deep amber color, 25 to 30 minutes. Let cool for 30 minutes before removing from the pan.

KATHERINE ALFORD

Apple-Maple Bread Pudding

Katherine is a well-known chef and food writer and a longtime friend who worked for me as assistant manager of Greenmarket. This dessert is an exciting take on an old-fashioned bread pudding and is one of those things that warms up your kitchen and fills it with delectable aromas.

For best results, use a medium- or soft-textured bread.

Makes 10 servings

2	cups whole milk
2	cups heavy cream
3/4	cup maple syrup
2	whole cloves
1	cinnamon stick
10	large eggs
4	tablespoons butter, plus extra for buttering the pan
4	large baking apples, such as Mutsu, peeled, cored, and sliced 1/8 to 1/4 inch thick
	Half a 1-pound loaf of bread sliced 1/3 inch thick, slices cut in half diagonally

Preheat the oven to 325°F. Place the milk, cream, maple syrup, cloves, and cinnamon stick in a medium saucepan over medium heat and bring to just under a boil. *Do not boil.* Let steep for 10 minutes.

Break the eggs into a large mixing bowl and beat well. Whisk in a little of the milk mixture to warm the eggs, then beat in the remainder of the milk mixture.

In a large skillet over medium heat, melt the butter. Add the apples and cook, stirring occasionally, until softened and golden, about 8 minutes.

Butter a 9-inch-round by 3-inch-deep earthenware baking dish and place the bread slices on the bottom to cover without crowding. Cover evenly with half the apples. Repeat the layers, ending with a third layer of bread. Strain the milk mixture over all.

Place the pan in a roasting pan and add hot water to come halfway up its sides. Bake until the pudding is set, about 40 minutes. Let cool at least 1 hour.

TRACEY SEAMAN

Toasted Pecan Waffles

Tracey Seaman, a talented food writer and recipe tester, travels to the Union Square Greenmarket from the far reaches of New Jersey. Her sure hand is responsible for the accuracy of many of the recipes included in this book.

This rather thin batter that she makes with plain whole milk yogurt and honey from Greenmarket stands can be used for both traditional waffles and pancakes. Serve with maple syrup and fresh fruit—the best the market has to offer. Whipped egg whites add lightness and ground toasted nuts add richness.

If necessary, warm cold eggs in their shells in a bowl of warm water, and bring the yogurt to room temperature by heating gently in the microwave.

1 1/3	cups pecan halves
2	large eggs, at room temperature, separated
2	cups plain whole milk yogurt, at room temperature
3	tablespoons honey
1 3/4	cups all-purpose flour
1 1/2	teaspoons baking soda
1/2	teaspoon salt
3	tablespoons unsalted butter, melted
	Pure maple syrup and sliced seasonal fruit, for serving

Makes 4 to 6 servings

Preheat the oven to 375°F. Place the pecans on a baking sheet and roast in the hot oven for 8 to 10 minutes, until nicely toasted. Transfer to a plate and let cool. When cool, place a generous 1/3 cup of the nuts in a food processor and process in long pulses until finely ground.

Meanwhile, preheat a waffle iron or griddle. In a medium bowl, whisk together the egg yolks, yogurt, and honey. Set aside.

In a large bowl, whisk together the flour, ground nuts, baking soda, and salt. In a second large bowl, whip the egg whites with a balloon whisk or electric mixer until stiff but not dry.

Add the yogurt mixture to the flour mixture, stirring just until incorporated. Gently fold in the egg whites until no streaks remain, then fold in the melted butter.

Make each waffle batch or pancake with 1/3 cup of batter, cooking until nicely golden. Top each serving with some of the remaining toasted nuts, and the maple syrup and fruit.

TRACEY SEAMAN

Crimson Chocolate Cake

The secret to the deep devil's food color of this moist and wonderful chocolate cake is the shredded raw beets and carrots folded into the batter. If desired, decorate the top of the cake with chocolate shavings.

FOR THE CAKE

5	small fresh beets (8 to 10 ounces), trimmed and peeled
2	medium carrots, scrubbed
2	ounces unsweetened chocolate
1½	cups all-purpose flour
½	cup unsweetened cocoa
2	teaspoons baking soda
2	teaspoons baking powder
¼	teaspoon salt
4	large eggs, at room temperature
2	cups sugar
2	teaspoons vanilla extract
⅔	cup vegetable oil

Makes 8 to 10 servings

Preheat the oven to 350°F. Lightly grease two 9-inch round cake pans.

Shred the beets and carrots through the grating disk of a food processor or with a box grater and reserve.

Place the chocolate in a small microwave-proof bowl and microwave at medium power for 1 minute. Stir, then cook at medium for 1 to 1½ minutes more. Stir until smooth.

In a bowl, whisk together the flour, cocoa, baking soda, baking powder, and salt.

In another large bowl, whisk together the eggs, sugar, and vanilla. Beat in the oil, mixing well until incorporated. Whisk in the melted chocolate; with a rubber spatula, stir in the flour mixture just until blended. Fold in the beets and carrots.

Scrape the batter evenly into the prepared cake pans. Bake in the middle of the oven until the layers are springy to the touch when pressed in the center, about 40 minutes. Let cool for 5 minutes in the pans set on racks; then turn out of the pans onto the racks and let cool completely.

FOR THE FROSTING

8	ounces semisweet chocolate, preferably imported, finely chopped
2½	cups heavy cream
2	teaspoons vanilla extract

Begin making the frosting while the cake is baking, or make it up to 2 days ahead.

In a medium saucepan over low heat, melt half of the semisweet chocolate in the cream, stirring until smooth. Remove from the heat and add the remaining chocolate; let stand for 2 minutes, then stir until smooth. Stir in the vanilla. Scrape into a large metal bowl, cover with plastic wrap, and refrigerate until well chilled, 3 hours or up to 2 days.

TO ASSEMBLE

Using an electric mixer, beat the cold chocolate frosting until thickened and spreadable. Invert one of the cake layers on a cake platter. Spread ¾ cup of the frosting on top. Place the second layer right side up on top, and spread the remaining frosting over the top and sides of the cake.

For best results, frost the cake within 3 hours of serving. The frosted cake can be wrapped in plastic and kept at room temperature for 1 day; refrigerate any leftovers, covered.

Spring

Spring surprises us with its gentle arrival at Greenmarket. For weeks, it seems, change has been in the air, along with the feeling that we've survived the winter, rested and regrouped, and are ready to start again. Everyone is antsy, they want to move, to get busy with the work and the fun of the new season. Customers seem to be coming out of the woodwork, greeting the farmers with "Hi, where have you been?" And many of the farmers reply: "I've been right here. Where have *you* been?"

Spring

As the spring days gradually warm up, farmers and market managers peel off the heavy jackets that they arrived in at dawn. Hot cider stands close, and Ronnybrook Farms doesn't sell much hot chocolate once the morning chill has lifted.

The season begins with the arrival of what I call the wild things of spring: tender greens like lamb's quarters, watercress, ramps, and fiddleheads. Like a lot of the produce that comes to Greenmarket, they started out as survival food and now are considered delicacies.

Ramps are the prime example of this evolution. Also called wild leeks, they look like a cross between a lily of the valley and a scallion, with a round bulb bottom and a little root, a white stalk that shades to red, and deep-green leaves that fan out on top. They have a sweet, garlicky, herbaceous taste. Towns in the south, midwest, and east hold yearly ramp festivals celebrating their complex, wonderful flavor. A friend who grew up in Ohio told me that during ramp season, you could be sent home from grade school if you smelled like you had overindulged. The pores of a ramp enthusiast exude the pungent odors of sweet onion and garlic.

Early spring also may bring broccoli and broccoli rabe to the market. If there has been a good snow cover during the winter, they will have grown through the cold months, a process known as "wintering over." Then farmers can bring them to us in the spring, sustaining us until it's time for the true summer harvest.

Color starts coming back everywhere, slowly at first, then with a bang. The delicate pink of fresh strawberries turns into bright red, and pale asparagus deepens to dark green.

Spring coincides with the Jewish holiday of Passover, which gives it special meaning for me. My grandfather had always been in charge of providing horseradish for the seder, the ceremonial dinner that marks the first two nights of the holiday. A whole root was needed for the symbolic seder plate, and his special grated horseradish always accompanied the sweet gefilte fish prepared by my grandmother. Freshly dug horseradish root was essential but wasn't easily available in suburbia years ago. But I was able to get some for my grandfather from Greenmarket farmers, and he experienced such joy in grating the pungent root for us by hand. Once he uncovered the bowl of his home-made horseradish in the kitchen, it took only seconds for its sharp, delicious smell to permeate the house.

Filling Your Market Basket in Spring
April, May, June

Blossoms	Cut Flowers	Ornamental Garden Starters	Edible Garden Starters
Forsythia	Daffodil	Impatiens	Herbs
Apple	Tulip	Petunia	Cucumber
Quince	Lily of the Valley	Geranium	Edible flowers
Cherry	Allium	Marigold	Hot and Sweet Peppers
Magnolia	Larkspur	Begonia	Lettuce
Dogwood	Sweet William	Dahlia	Salad greens
Lilac	Lavender	New Guinea Impatiens	Tomato
		Pansy	Strawberry

Herbs
Chamomile
Chervil
Lemon Balm
Chives
Chive Blossom
Lovage
Lavender
Dill
Cilantro
French Tarragon

Edible Flowers
Viola
Johnny Jump-Up
Zucchini Blossom

Lettuce
Batavian or French
  (Canasta)
Butterhead or Bibb
  (Brune d'Hiver)
Crisphead or Iceberg
  (Chou de Naples)
Cos or Romaine (Little
  Gem)
Looseleaf (Black-Seeded
  Simpson)

Salad and Cooking Greens
Wild Watercress

Lamb's Quarters
Baby Mustard
Baby Dandelion
Miner's Lettuce
Mâche
Arugula
Radicchio (Italian
  Chicory)
Spinach
Sorrel
Red Amaranth
Baby Pac Choi
Swiss Chard
Broccoli Rabe (Rapini)
Curly Endive (Frisée)
Collard
Dandelion (Red or Green)
Baby Kale
Mizuna
Mustard

Vegetables
Fiddlehead Fern (Ostrich
  Fern)
Asparagus
Snow Pea
Sugar Snap Pea (Sugar
  Pea)
English Pea (Shelling or
  Green Pea)
Rhubarb

Cultivated Mushrooms
Button
Cremini
Portobello
Shiitake

Wild Mushrooms
Morel
Chanterelle
Oyster (Tree Mushroom,
  Hiratake)

Root Crops
Ramp (Wild Leek)
Scallion
Leek
Horseradish
Parsnip
Parsley Root
Burdock (Gobo)
Spring Onion
Jerusalem Artichoke
  (Sunchoke)
Salsify (Oyster Plant)
New Red Potato
Radish: Red; White Ici-
  cle; Easter Egg;
  French Breakfast;
  Hailstone

Fruit
Apple
Strawberry
Cherry: Sweet; Sour (Pie)

Eggs
Chicken
Duck
Goose
Pheasant
Wild Turkey
Guinea Hen

Poultry, Meat, and Game
Chicken
Cornish Game Hen
Soup Pheasant

Fish and Seafood
Boston Mackerel
Gray Sole (Flounder)
Porgy
Sea Bass
Shad
Whiting
Freshwater Trout
Oysters
Clams
Crab
Smoked Fish

Also available in spring
  are dried flowers and
  grasses; honey; maple
  syrup (spring is a new
  maple syrup season);
  grains, such as corn-
  meal, buckwheat
  groats, rye, and wheat
  berries; prepared
  products, such as
  cider and jams; and
  seasonal baked prod-
  ucts, such as straw-
  berry-rhubarb pie.

Lucas, the coolest rhubarb
salesperson at Greenmarket

Spring

Spring Recipes

Fred Wilklow, Wilklow Farms

Once, on a drizzly spring morning just before Mother's Day, I helped Fred Wilklow, a Hudson Valley farmer, and his family bunch lilacs in the back of their truck. Undeterred by the rain and shoulder deep in beautiful lilacs, Fred described what an orchardist likes to see as spring progresses. He talked about how the young fruit emerge one after the other in his orchards: first the apricots, then early plums, then cherries, followed by later plums, peaches, and apples. Fred watches day by day, in some cases hour by hour, to see how the weather will affect all his delicate crops.

Strawberries

The first harvest of tart strawberries makes for many red-stained, puckered lips as thousands of New Yorkers sample the slightly unripe crimson jewels.

"How's the sugar?" a chef calls out to my wife, Marry, who is building a massive display of strawberries in quart and pint containers for Ray and Sue Dare of Cherry Lane Farms.

Customers chime in: "Do I want the pink ones or the dark red ones?" "Pick out the best ones for me."

Sue busily offers advice: "Try one from this basket, they're the sweetest!"

During the next few weeks, the puckers will turn to smiles as the berries ripen, deepen in color, and achieve that luscious balance of sugar and acid that makes one quart of strawberries never enough to put in your market basket. The best recipe for the sweet, ripe berries? Eat them with your fingers, on the way home. If any are left, serve them in a bowl with nothing added.

Ray ("Bunk") and Susan Dare

Ray Dare

Ray Dare, Jr., is a fifth-generation farmer who grew up working on his dad's Cherry Lane Farms in Bridgeton, New Jersey.

Some years ago an older farmer, Willis Fleetwood, was visiting the Dares. Ray asked him how he determined when the last hard frost was past and it would be safe to set tomato plants outside. Fleetwood pointed to a stand of wild dogwood. "You see those trees? When they're in bloom, you know the frost is past. They are the smartest trees in the world." Ever since, Ray has used the dogwood trees as his fail-safe and has never lost a tomato plant to frost.

In the early 1980s, when Ray was selling strawberries at his pick-your-own stand, he was told that Frank Stiles, another farmer, had sold 2,000 quarts in one day at Greenmarket. Not surprisingly, by the next season, Ray was selling at Greenmarket, too. He started at West Seventy-seventh Street with his friend and then-partner Morris Kernan ("Kerney"). They drove up from South Jersey at six-thirty A.M. on a Sunday, with 1,200 quarts of berries, and then just sat there! Ray described the debacle: "It was a very hot day and we didn't have a canopy. Our table legs were melting into the blacktop. The fruit in my truck began to melt and strawberry juice was running out of the floor drains in the pickup onto the ground." By the time the market closed they had sold only half their load.

But the next week they came prepared. They protected the fruit with a large canopy, brought only half the amount of berries, and added some asparagus to their table display. They did better.

Their reputation for quality produce grew quickly, and soon they were offered a spot at the World Trade Center market. Frank Stiles (he of the early Greenmarket success) called to offer some cultural advice: "Bunch the aspara-gus—city people won't buy it loose."

"By seven A.M. the doors to the World Trade Center opened and I knew I had a market," Ray says. They sold out almost everything by two P.M., but stayed on until the truck was completely empty.

MARKET PEOPLE
Ron Binaghi, Jr.

Chefs love to hang out and chat at Ron Binaghi, Jr.'s, Stokes Farm stand, while they shop for aromatic fresh herbs for their restaurant kitchens. Some tell me that it gives them a chance to catch their breath before heading back to work. What better place to inhale than at the herb stand?

Ron remembers his early experiences at New York's first Greenmarket, at Fifty-ninth Street and Second Avenue, in 1976:

"I was intimidated by the big city. I didn't know what we needed—scales, bags, change, or whatever. We learned some crazy lessons from our own mistakes. On rainy days, people shopped with the water running over their shoes in the gravel parking lot. They even came out in storms, and during a particularly bad one, all the rainwater that had ac-cumulated on our canopy came down at once. It just missed a woman's head, but it sure filled her pocketbook.

"In the city, we saw homeless people for the first time, and it was a real eye-opener. Now we donate food to them—we realize how much we have when we meet others with significantly less."

A Child's Garden of Herbs

One of the pleasures of my job is cohosting, along with other market managers, tour groups of school kids. These tours are always ener-getic, often riotous, and it's hard to say who enjoys them more, the kids or the managers. Stokes Farm herb stand is always a big hit.

I tell the kids to close their eyes and roll the leaves of a freshly cut herb between their fingers. I don't tell them which one it is—they will have to guess.

Once they've rolled, I ask

Ron Binaghi, jr.

them to bring the crushed leaves up to their noses. Now the guessing begins.

Soap!

The stuff Mommy rubs on Daddy's back when it's sore!

Candy!

The dentist!

Toothpaste!

Mouthwash!

Gum!

Tea!

Ice cream!

Easter at my uncle's house!

Our conclusion: it's mint. And it's everywhere.

Herb Chart

A generation ago, fresh basil, most likely a Genovese or Neapolitan type, was found only in specialty stores or backyard gardens. The real world gets smaller every day, but not our world, agriculture, which gets bigger each season. That is why today any good farmers' market in America will offer shoppers a global tour on the wings of freshly cut basil and many other enticing herbs.

What a pleasure it is to buy herbs at Greenmarket, where they are tied into fragrant bunches (usually from 2 to 4 ounces) or sold loose—not forced into little trays and wrapped in plastic. Take as many whiffs as you please and let yourself be tempted.

USING HERBS

Chef Peter Hoffman: Add herbs toward the end of the cooking time. By doing this, you will keep the brightness of the herb. Chef Gray Kunz: I like all varieties of *basil*—green, purple, lemon, Thai. I prefer to use the whole leaf. Some favorite uses are in salads and stocks, such as Thai basil in shrimp stock. I like *winter savory* with green beans. Farmer Anne Salomon: Make a pesto base with *summer savory, parsley, tarragon, thyme, and garlic.* Use *shiso* in a marinade for chicken or lamb. Chef Bill Telepan: Try *black mint* instead of basil in marinated tomato salads. Use *tarragon* in a simple sauté of mushrooms and shallots. Use *chervil* in fresh mayonnaise. Sauté *summer savory* with corn kernels, butter, and mushrooms. *Thyme* is the mother herb that brings all other herbs together. *Sage* is excellent cooked with browned butter and served over pasta, such as ravioli made with sheep's milk. A *chamomile* infusion can be served as a dressing for cold fish salads or cold lobster dishes:

1/2 cup chamomile flowers
1/2 cup canola oil
     Zest of 1 lemon

Crush the flowers and mix with oil and zest in a small saucepan. Simmer over low heat for 3 hours. Let cool; strain.

Try a *lavender* glaze on roasted duck:

1/2 cup honey
1/2 cup sherry vinegar
 2 sprigs lavender

Place all ingredients in a saucepan and cook over medium-low heat until reduced to a syrup. Let cool; strain.

Description

Anise Hyssop A member of the mint family. Square, boxy stems; thin, cone-shaped, purple blossoms; long, pointy leaves. Sweet, aniselike flavor.

Basil Flavor and appearance differ among varieties: *Anise (Thai, Oriental, Licorice)* strong licorice aroma and flavor. *Cinnamon* spicy cinnamon aroma and flavor with hints of clove. *Fino (Piccolo)* intensely sweet and aromatic; small leaves. *Genovese* highly perfumed; strong basil flavor. *Lemon* green leaves; distinctly lemony scent and flavor. *Opal (Purple)* milder scent and flavor than green types. *Napoletano* dreamy, sweet fragrance; mellow flavor.

Bee Balm (Bergamot, Oswego Tea) Native to eastern U.S. After the Boston Tea Party, the colonists brewed Oswego tea instead of the real stuff.

Borage (Cool Tankard) Light purplish-blue blossoms; leaves and blossoms have a cucumber-like flavor.

Chamomile Yellow, apple-scented flowers.

Catnip Fragrant gray-green leaves.

Chervil Soft-green, lacy leaves. Flavor is a delicate blend of flat-leaf parsley and licorice. Popular but hard to grow and hard to find, even in farmers' markets.

Chives A member of the onion family. Long green hollow stems; delicate, sweet, onionlike flavor. Blossoms, resembling large purple clover flowers, are sold in late spring and early fall.

Let's Eat!

Use blossoms as salad garnish. Both blossoms and leaves make a cooling tea, are good in ice cream and dessert sauces, and go well with rich meats.

Use all types in pestos, salads, salsas, pastas, rice dishes, curries, fish or poultry dishes. Layer with slices of mozzarella and ripe tomatoes. *Anise* use with poultry and fish; popular in Southeast Asian dishes. *Cinnamon* good in marinades, chutney, jellies. *Fino* excellent in pesto. *Genovese* use in tomato salads, cooked sauces; good for drying. *Lemon* perfect in soups, with rice dishes, and grilled fish. *Opal* excellent in flavored vinegars or as salad garnishes. *Napoletano* use in salads, pesto, cooked dishes.

Use as a garnish; in salads and dessert sauces; to flavor jellies; as tea.

Use the blossoms as a garnish in salads and summer beverages. Young leaves and blossoms can replace cucumbers in any uncooked dish; mix with sour cream as a sauce for smoked fish. Stems, leaves, and blossoms can be made into fritters.

Used in teas, other summer beverages, and in vinaigrettes for seafood salads.

Place blossoms and leaves inside an old sock, tie the end, and toss it to your cats. For humans, makes a calming tea.

Excellent raw or cooked. Component of French fines herbes (along with chives, parsley, and tarragon); use in broths and infusions. Blends well with mayonnaise.

Stems are good stuffed in trout, wrapped around fish steak or filet. Blossoms are good in salads.

Spring

Description	**Let's Eat!**
Cilantro (Chinese Parsley) Seeds sold as coriander seeds. Resembles flat-leaf parsley; pungent aroma and flavor.	Use in salsas, pesto, guacamole. Popular in Middle Eastern, Indian, Asian, Latin American, Southwestern U.S., and Caribbean cuisines; roots used in Thai cuisine.
Dill Blue-green feathery leaves when young; stalks topped by tiny yellow flowers when older.	Used for pickling, especially Kirby cucumbers. Goes well with beets, beans, carrots, eggs, summer squash, fish, seafood, egg salad, chicken soup.
Epazote Flat, pointed leaves; pungent smell and strong, sour flavor. Ron says: "It smells like bleach!"	Popular in Mexican cuisine; often combined with Mexican oregano. Cooked with beans, it reduces the flatulence they can cause.
French Tarragon Sparse blue-green leaves on narrow stems; bright, licorice flavor (not to be confused with the less flavorful Russian tarragon).	May be used in salads and cooked dishes; good with sauteed mushrooms; used to flavor vinegar. A component of fines herbes.
Garlic Chives (Chinese or Oriental Chives) Resemble chives, but are a different botanical species. Taste is mild blend of garlic and chives. White blossoms are sometimes sold.	Has the same uses as chives.
Lavender Spiked foliage; tall, fragrant blossoms; colors include cloud white, powder blue, deep purple, and lavender. Many varieties, some with a blend of piney and smoky scent, some pure perfume. Leaves and stems are as fragrant as the blooms.	Used in perfumes and sachets. Makes refreshing tea, dessert sauce, ice cream, sorbet. Dried, rolled leaves can be used as incense.
Lemongrass Thin, light-green, papery leaves rising out of a scallion-type base. Blends sour lemon and sweet flavors.	Leaves are used to flavor soups, curries, fish dishes, and teas. (Discard leaves before serving.) Peeled and chopped (or crushed) base is used in stir-fried dishes and sauces.
Lovage (Smallage, Smellage) Resembles a large, many-branched celery, with leaves jutting out from the stalks. Strong, pungent celerylike flavor and aroma, but deeper and more savory, with hints of anise and juniper berries.	Use sparingly. Popular ingredient in Eastern European soups, goulash, fish dishes. Ron says: "My Romanian customers buy lovage. They whisper, 'Hey, my friend, you have the lovage?' like it was black market."

Description	Let's Eat!

Marjoram A close relative of oregano, Anne calls it "the king of oreganos." Gray-green small, tight flowers and stems. Flavor is subtler and sweeter than oregano.

Used when a light touch is called for in cooked dishes, such as eggs, vegetables, fish, and meats; Ron says, "Great in stew."

Mint All varieties have boxy stems and leaves that branch out at irregular intervals. Both stems and leaves may range from light to dark green to deep purple. *Apple Mint* Medium-size rounded leaves; a delicate blend of apples and spearmint. *Black Peppermint (English Black Peppermint)* Sturdy purple and green stems; leaves of dark green dabbed with purple. Deep peppermint taste and aroma. *Blue Balsam* Shiny, dark-green leaves with a purple tint; more flavorful than peppermint. *Candy* Glossy, round leaves and a sweet scent reminiscent of Life Savers candy. *Chocolate Peppermint* Dark-green leaves; peppermint scent; rich flavor with chocolate overtones. *Doublemint* Two mints in one—spearmint taste and peppermint background. *Eau de Cologne* Rounded, dark-green leaves; sweet flavor; very fragrant.

All mint can be used in salads, seafood and poultry dishes, beverages, jellies, and with vegetables and grains.

Ron says: "We sell a ton of mint on the Saturday of the Kentucky Derby. People want mint juleps for the race."

Oregano Bright-green, small leaves; pungent flavor and aroma. *Greek, Italian,* and *Spanish* are the most popular varieties; flavors and aromas range from light and warm to earthy and strong. Avoid any that are bitter or acidic. Dried herb that is sold in stores is usually a mixture of several types.

Goes well with tomatoes, meat, fish. Use in tomato sauces and any cooked dishes.

Parsley *Curly* has small, frilly leaves and mild flavor; *Flat-leaf* or *Italian* has broader, flat leaves and a warm, refreshing flavor.

Component of fines herbes and bouquet garni. *Curly* is used mainly as a garnish. *Flat-leaf* goes well with any fresh or cooked dish.

Rosemary Green, needle-shaped leaves. When extremely fresh, leaves are resin coated. Sharp, piney flavor; honey and pine aroma.

Use with lamb, chicken, vegetables, potatoes. Anne makes iced rosemary tea and rosemary sorbet. Use long branches as skewers for grilling.

Sage Silver-gray-green leaves; musty fragrance.

Used in pestos, sauces; with meats and vegetables; good in brown-butter sauces. Anne suggests batter-fried leaves. Sage is used in some religious ceremonies, such as Native American.

Spring

Description	Let's Eat!
Savory, Winter and Summer Varieties Tiny, pointed green leaves. *Winter Savory* has strong hints of rosemary and mint; *Summer Savory,* of oregano and marjoram.	*Winter* goes well with roasted pork; *Winter* and *Summer* go well with summer vegetables.
Shiso (Perilla, Beefsteak Leaves) The quintessential Japanese herb. Large green or purple leaves; grassy flavor with mint-lemon undertones.	An acquired taste for some. Used to garnish sashimi. Good in pesto, combined with basil.
Thyme Many varieties. Tiny, oval, pointed, shiny leaves; many-branched stems. Aromatic and strong flavored. *Variegated Lemon Thyme* has citrus flavor. *English Thyme* has pungent flavor.	Good with rice, fish, chicken. Anne likes thyme with candied carrots.
Verbena (Lemon Verbena) Long, slender, green leaves, subtle lemony scent and flavor.	Good in anything that goes with lemon: vinaigrette, tea, sorbet, granita; try it mixed into softened vanilla ice cream.

MARKET PEOPLE
Tony Mannetta

In June 1984, we opened a market on a service road outside the World Trade Center and I was assigned to manage it. Farmers arrived at the crack of dawn and set up breathtaking displays, but that morning, the Trade Center employees walked past them on their way to work and just looked puzzled.

Farmers were concerned. Had we miscalculated? Would office employees bother to lug produce back to their offices? By lunchtime, however, most stands were swamped with people in crowds four or five deep. I was delighted—the market had been discovered.

I waded into the crowd and yelled to one grower, "Isn't this great?" He shouted back, "Hell, no! They ain't buying a thing. They're just staring at me. I feel like a monkey in the zoo!"

I looked around. People were pressed against the tables, the ones in the rear pressed against those in front. Everyone was just staring. I asked a man in a business suit standing next to me: "What's going on here?" He replied, "I don't know, I think it's a movie shoot. They have these produce stands set up for some shoot."

It dawned on me that all these people had never been to an urban farmers' market. Jumping on top of the nearest empty vegetable crate, I shouted to the crowd: "Welcome to Greenmarket, New York's farmers' market! The people behind the stands are farmers. The produce is fresh picked and is for sale!"

That was all it took. People started buying, and grins broke out as customers bit into field-ripe strawberries for the first time. Executives, secretaries, service workers could all be seen taking away bags of peaches, corn, collards, tomatoes—you name it. The workers were thrilled; the farmers were ecstatic.

ALAN HARDING
Chilled Cucumber Soup

Chef Alan Harding of Patois has given us a very simple recipe—I can't stress how simple—for a fresh-tasting chilled cucumber soup. As in Indian cuisine, the yogurt base is enhanced with cardamom and curry, very refreshing in the spring, and cooling later, in the heat of summer.

8	medium cucumbers, all but 1 peeled and coarsely chopped
$1/4$	cup fresh lemon juice
2	teaspoons kosher salt
$1/4$	teaspoon freshly ground pepper
2	tablespoons white wine vinegar
$1^1/2$	teaspoons hot curry powder
	Pinch cardamom
	Pinch cayenne
1	cup plain yogurt

Makes 4 servings

Place the chopped cucumbers, the lemon juice, salt, pepper, vinegar, curry powder, cardamom, and cayenne in a blender and puree. Pass through a fine strainer into a large bowl and whisk in the yogurt. Season with salt and pepper.

Quarter the remaining cucumber lengthwise, seed, and thinly slice. Garnish with the cucumber slices.

WALDY MALOUF

Potato and Sorrel Soup with Red Pepper Cream

This is a soup for spring, especially if you can find some ramps to use with the sorrel. Ramps are pungent wild members of the onion family; they taste like a combination of onions, leeks, scallions, chives, and garlic, and add a distinctively piquant flavor to the already tangy sorrel. This soup is equally good hot or cold (you may add cream to the chilled soup, if you like) and, like almost all soups, improves with age—make it a day or two ahead.

FOR THE POTATO AND SORREL SOUP

4	tablespoons unsalted butter
1	pound ramps, cleaned and coarsely chopped, or 6 slender leeks, including 2 inches of the green part, cleaned and thinly sliced
2	celery ribs, thinly sliced
2	medium onions, thinly sliced
1½	pounds baking potatoes, peeled and sliced
½	pound sorrel, shredded (about 4 cups)
12	cups chicken stock (or vegetable stock)
1	cup heavy cream (optional, for serving cold)
	Coarse salt and freshly ground pepper

Makes 8 servings

Melt the butter in a 6- to 8-quart, heavy-bottomed soup pot over medium heat and cook the ramps, celery, and onions, stirring often, until wilted but not browned, about 8 minutes. Add the potatoes and shredded sorrel and stir well. Pour in the stock, bring to a boil, and simmer partially covered for 1 hour, until the potatoes are very tender. Run the mixture through a food mill or press through a sieve. Let it cool completely. Stir in the cream, if using, add the salt and pepper, and refrigerate, covered, up to 2 days.

FOR THE RED PEPPER CREAM

1	roasted red bell pepper (see page 15)
½	cup heavy cream

Puree the prepared pepper in a blender or food processor.

In a small bowl, whip the cream until soft, fold in the pepper puree, and season with salt and pepper. Continue whipping until the cream is stiff.

Potato and sorrel soup
1   cup finely chopped sorrel for garnish, optional
Red pepper puree or cream
1/2   cup heavy cream, optional

Reheat the soup and stir in the chopped sorrel. Float a rounded tablespoon of red pepper cream on each bowl of soup. To serve chilled, stir the chopped sorrel into the cold soup, add heavy cream, if desired, and top each serving with the red bell pepper puree.

HERB TIPS

Growing   Farmer Ron Binaghi, Jr.: *Mint* is easy to grow and hard to kill. If it's planted in a pot, be sure it is by itself, since the roots travel underground and like to take over their neighbors. To prevent total invasion, cut both ends off a coffee can and sink it 3 inches into the ground. Plant the mint in the top of the can and hope that you've outsmarted it. (However, mint has a way of finding new areas to invade.) *Chives* are the easiest herb to grow at home. They can be outside all year, and even freeze solid in a small pot, and be ready to cut again in spring.   **Buying**   Herbs should be fragrant. They should have no brown leaves or browning at the bottom of the bunch.   **Storing**   Wrap fresh herbs in damp paper towels, wrap in plastic, and refrigerate.

DIANE FORLEY
Sorrel Soup with Potherb Dumplings

This wonderful spring recipe reminds me of my grandmother's soup with knaidlach—*matzo-meal dumplings. Chef Diane Forley of Verbena Restaurant gives us a soup that is tangy and lemony, with the bonus of light-as-air dumplings made from herbs, spinach, and ricotta—and a touch of matzo meal.*

FOR THE SORREL SOUP

- 2 tablespoons olive oil
- 1 large onion, finely diced
- 2 leeks, trimmed, split, rinsed, and finely diced
- 1/4 pound sorrel (about 3 cups)
- 2 quarts water or vegetable stock
- 1/4 pound spinach (about 4 cups packed)
- 1 tablespoon lemon juice
- 2 teapoons lemon zest (from 1 to 2 lemons)
- Salt and freshly ground black pepper

Makes 6 to 8 servings

Heat the olive oil in a 4- to 6-quart Dutch oven over medium heat. Add the onion and leeks and cook, stirring occasionally, until softened and translucent but not colored, about 12 minutes. Stir in the sorrel and cook until it begins to break apart, about 5 minutes. Add the water, spinach, lemon juice, and zest and cook until the spinach is wilted, about 3 minutes. Season with salt and pepper. Process with a handheld blender or in a food processor or blender until just pureed.

FOR THE POTHERB DUMPLINGS

$1^1/_2$ cups chives (cut in 1-inch lengths)

$^2/_3$ cup tarragon leaves

6 cups parsley leaves

2 cups ricotta cheese

2 large eggs

2 large egg whites

$1/_3$ cup grated Parmesan cheese, plus extra for garnish, if desired

Pinch of grated nutmeg

$1/_2$ teaspoon kosher salt

$1/_4$ teaspoon freshly ground pepper

$1/_2$ cup flour

$1^1/_2$ cups matzo meal

Put the chives, tarragon, and parsley in a food processor and mince. Add the ricotta, eggs, egg whites, Parmesan, nutmeg, salt, pepper, flour, and matzo meal and process until well mixed.

Shape into 1- by $1/_2$-inch ovals with your hands. Place on a sheet pan and refrigerate about $1/_2$ hour.

Bring a 1-quart saucepan of salted water to just under a boil and cook the dumplings in batches until cooked through, about 5 minutes each batch. Divide them among 6 to 8 soup bowls and ladle the sorrel soup over the top. (The dumplings are best eaten immediately.) Sprinkle with grated Parmesan, if desired.

BILL TELEPAN
Fried Green Tomato Salad with Goat Cheese

Chef Bill Telepan of JUdson Grill has a real talent for using seasonal ingredients. The subtle garlic vinaigrette enhances the flavors of the fresh tomatoes and sharp goat cheese in this beautiful layered salad.

FOR THE TOMATOES

2	cups corn flour (finely ground cornmeal)
1/2	teaspoon salt
1/8	teaspoon freshly ground black pepper
2	eggs beaten with 2 tablespoons water
2	large green tomatoes (1 1/2 pounds), each cut into 6 slices
2	cups olive oil

Makes 4 servings

In a medium bowl, toss together the corn flour, salt, and pepper. Dip the tomatoes in the egg wash, then coat well with the corn flour. Set aside on a plate.

Pour 1/2 inch olive oil into a large cast-iron skillet over medium heat and heat until very hot. In batches, without crowding, pan fry the tomatoes, turning once, until golden brown, about 6 minutes, then drain on paper towels.

FOR THE SALAD

8	ounces goat cheese
1	teaspoon chopped fresh thyme
1	tablespoon milk
	Coarse salt
	Freshly ground pepper
1	garlic clove, minced and mashed into a paste
1/2	teaspoon Tabasco sauce
1	teaspoon Worcestershire sauce
2	tablespoons fresh lemon juice
1/2	cup olive oil
6	cups (4 ounces) mesclun greens

In a mixing bowl, stir together the goat cheese, thyme, milk, and salt and pepper, to taste, until blended. Set aside.

To make the dressing, in a small bowl, whisk together the garlic paste,

Tabasco sauce, Worcestershire sauce, and lemon juice, and season with salt, and pepper. Whisk in the olive oil and adjust the seasoning.

In a large bowl, toss the greens with the dressing. Divide among 4 plates. On each plate, layer 3 tomato slices with 2 tablespoons goat cheese mixture between the layers, next to the mesclun. Drizzle any remaining dressing on top.

John Adams

DAVID PAGE

David's Creamy Potato Salad

David Page and his wife, Barbara Shinn, own Home and Drovers Tap Room restaurants, as well as the takeout shop, Home Away From Home, where they use farm-fresh Greenmarket ingredients.

This is the kind of potato salad I like best, with no mayonnaise to hide the fresh flavors of potatoes and herbs. The chef advises you to sneak as much of it for yourself as possible.

2	pounds small red or yellow potatoes, as fresh as possible, quartered
8	garlic cloves
5	tablespoons apple cider vinegar
5	tablespoons olive oil
2	tablespoons chopped fresh herbs (such as basil or chives)
1	tablespoon crushed mustard seeds
1	teaspoon salt
1/4	teaspoon freshly ground pepper

Makes 6 servings

Place the potatoes and garlic in a large pot of salted water to cover and bring to a boil. Reduce the heat and simmer until fork tender, about 20 minutes. Drain and let cool to room temperature. Mash with a fork or masher until creamy but still chunky. Stir in the remaining ingredients. Serve with everything.

KEVIN JOHNSON

Strawberry and Baby Greens Salad with Strawberry Vinaigrette

The Grange Hall restaurant, for which Jay Saluich does most of the shopping and Kevin Johnson the cooking, highlights American farmland food and has a natural connection to Greenmarket. We in the Northeast used to think of June as strawberry season, but since the introduction of day-neutral strawberry varieties, luscious berries are available at Greenmarket from spring to the first hard frost.

FOR THE STRAWBERRY VINAIGRETTE

- 1/3 cup coarsely chopped strawberries
- 3 tablespoons fresh orange juice
- 1/3 cup olive oil
- 3 tablespoons white wine vinegar
- 1/4 teaspoon salt
  Freshly ground black pepper to taste
  Pinch sugar

Makes 6 servings

Place the strawberries, orange juice, olive oil, and vinegar in a blender or food processor and process until smooth. Season with salt, pepper, and sugar and refrigerate until chilled. (You will have about 3/4 cup.)

FOR THE SALAD

- 1/3 cup pine nuts
- 1/2 pound baby spinach, stemmed, rinsed, and dried (about 6 cups)
- 1/2 pound baby greens or mesclun mix, rinsed and dried (about 6 cups)
- 2/3 cup sliced strawberries
- 1 small red onion, peeled and thinly sliced

Preheat the oven to 350°F and toast the pine nuts on a baking sheet until golden, about 5 minutes. Let cool completely. Toss together the spinach and greens and divide among 6 salad plates. Top with the sliced strawberries and onion. Drizzle with the strawberry vinaigrette and sprinkle with the pine nuts.

DAN SILVERMAN
Ricotta Gnocchi with Local Asparagus and Ramps (Wild Leeks)

Dan Silverman, a loyal market supporter and talented New York City chef, gives us this recipe that makes use of ramps, or wild leeks. Mixing these full-flavored vegetables with shallots, asparagus, and delicate ricotta gnocchi is a great way to highlight spring.

FOR THE GNOCCHI
- 1 pound fresh ricotta
- 3 large eggs
- 1 cup all-purpose flour
- 1/2 teaspoon salt
- 1/4 teaspoon freshly ground pepper
- Pinch of freshly grated nutmeg

Makes 4 to 6 servings

Bring a large pot of salted water to a boil and reduce to a simmer.

Meanwhile, combine the ricotta cheese and eggs in a food processor or mixer and blend well. Add the flour, salt, pepper, and nutmeg and process until smooth and slightly stiff.

Using 2 teaspoons to form small ovals, gently drop spoonfuls of the mixture into the simmering water. Once the gnocchi rise to the surface, let them cook for 2 to 3 minutes. Cook in batches of 10 to 12, so they are not crowded in the pot. Remove the cooked gnocchi with a slotted spoon or skimmer, refresh in a bowl of cold water, and drain. Can be made up to 3 hours ahead; cover and refrigerate.

KEVIN JOHNSON

Buttered Sugar Snap Peas with Fresh Mint

This delightful dish from Chef Kevin Johnson of the Grange Hall restaurant is the color of spring. Aromatic fresh mint perfectly complements the crunchy sweet peas—remember, don't overcook your peas because you want that crunch. The only thing that could be easier would be eating the sugar snaps raw.

1	pound sugar snap peas, ends snapped to remove stems and strings
2	tablespoons unsalted butter
1/2	teaspoon salt
	Freshly ground pepper
1/4	cup coarsely chopped fresh mint

Makes 6 servings

Blanch the peas 1 minute in a pot of boiling salted water. In a large skillet over medium-high heat, melt the butter. Add the peas and stir until bright green and crisp-tender, about 3 minutes. Season with the salt and pepper to taste, toss with the mint, and serve hot.

CHRISTIAN ALBIN
Vegetable Pot au Feu with Ramp Vinaigrette

Christian Albin, executive chef at The Four Seasons Restaurant, gives us his Greenmarket, vegetarian version of a traditional French meat and vegetable stew. He combines ramps, celery roots (wintered over, they are available before the warmer weather), and baby golden beets, as well as asparagus, carrots, and parsnips. With all this farm-fresh flavor, meat is not at all missed.

FOR THE VEGETABLES

1	quart chicken or vegetable stock
1	jalapeño pepper
1	garlic clove
1	bay leaf
2	cloves
	Salt and freshly ground pepper
8	baby yellow beets
8	asparagus spears
2	medium carrots
10	ramps (wild leeks)
1	small celery root
4	medium shallots
1	medium white turnip
1	medium parsnip

Makes 4 servings

Bring the stock to a boil in a large pot and add the jalapeño pepper, garlic, bay leaf, cloves, and salt and pepper to taste. Reduce the heat, cover, and simmer about 15 minutes.

Meanwhile, peel the vegetables (except the ramps), trim, and cut into bite-size pieces. Add all the vegetables to the stock, reduce the temperature to low, and cook until the vegetables are tender.

Strain the stock and return it to the pot. Reserve the vegetables, keeping the ramps separate. Keep the stock and vegetables warm.

FOR THE RAMP VINAIGRETTE

10	cooked ramps (see above)
3	tablespoons red wine vinegar
	Salt and freshly ground pepper
1/2	cup extra virgin olive oil
1	tablespoon Dijon mustard
2	tablespoons sliced chives, for garnish

Place the ramps, vinegar, salt, and pepper in a blender and process until smooth. Strain through a fine sieve into a small bowl and whisk in the olive oil and mustard.

Divide the vegetables among 4 shallow bowls and ladle 1 cup of stock over each portion. Drizzle with ramp vinaigrette and garnish with the chives.

WALDY MALOUF

Asparagus with Morels

Asparagus and morels are the essence of spring, and this is an inspired combination from the world-famous chef Waldy Malouf. It reminds us of both the cultivated and the wild things of the season.

1 stick (8 tablespoons) unsalted butter
2 medium shallots, finely chopped
2 large garlic cloves, minced
1 teaspoon chopped fresh thyme, plus 6 sprigs for garnish
1 pound morels, cleaned and halved or quartered lengthwise
1 cup dry white wine
1 cup vegetable or chicken stock
  Salt and freshly ground pepper
1 pound asparagus, trimmed to 6 inches long

Makes 6 servings

In a large skillet over medium heat, melt 6 tablespoons of the butter. When the butter is hot but not browned, add the shallots and garlic, then sprinkle the thyme on top. Add the morels and cook until lightly browned, about 5 minutes, taking care not to burn the butter.

Pour in the wine and boil until it is almost evaporated, about 5 minutes. Add the stock, stir well, and simmer until the liquid is reduced and has thickened slightly. Season lightly with salt and pepper and swirl in the remaining 2 tablespoons butter. (You should have about 3 cups.)

Meanwhile, prepare the asparagus. If the spears are thicker than ½ inch in diameter, peel the bottom half of each with a vegetable peeler.

In a large skillet with a tight-fitting lid, bring ½ inch of water to a boil. Lay the asparagus in the pan, cover, and cook vigorously just until the bottom of a stalk can be pierced easily with a sharp knife, about 4 minutes. Drain on paper towels.

Divide among 6 dinner plates and spoon the morels across the middle of the asparagus, making sure that each serving includes 1 or 2 spoonfuls of the pan juices. Garnish each plate with a sprig of thyme and serve immediately.

Stuffed Flounder Rolls

Jack Gunn, known in the market as "Jack Flash," is a fisherman who sells his fresher-than-fresh catch to our lucky customers. Here is one of his favorite recipes for sweet flounder fillets.

1	pound button mushrooms, quartered
1	medium onion, coarsely chopped
1	teaspoon fresh lemon juice
1/4	cup olive oil
1/4	cup fresh breadcrumbs
	Kosher salt
	Freshly ground black pepper
8	small flounder or sole fillets (1 pound)
2/3	cup flour
1	garlic clove, peeled and crushed
2	medium tomatoes, peeled, seeded, and cut into 1/4-inch dice
1/4	cup dry white wine
1 1/2	teaspoons coarsely chopped fresh thyme leaves

Makes 4 servings

In a food processor, pulse the mushrooms and onion with the lemon juice until finely chopped.

In a medium skillet, heat 2 tablespoons of the oil over medium heat. Add the mushroom mixture and cook until most of the liquid evaporates, about 8 minutes. Stir in the breadcrumbs and salt and pepper to taste. Remove from the heat and set aside.

Lay the fillets out on a work surface and spread a heaping tablespoon of stuffing over each one. Roll each fillet into a loose cylinder and secure with a toothpick. Coat each roll with flour.

Heat the remaining 2 tablespoons of oil in a large nonstick skillet over medium-high heat. Add the fish rolls and reduce the heat to medium. Cook, turning occasionally, until browned on each side, about 5 minutes. Remove to a serving plate and cover to keep warm.

Add the garlic to the skillet and cook, stirring, until golden, about 2 minutes. Add the tomatoes, wine, and thyme. Bring to a boil over high heat, stirring continuously until the liquid is reduced by half and the tomatoes are soft, about 4 minutes. Season with salt and pepper to taste.

Spoon the sauce over the fish rolls and serve immediately.

CHARLES KIELY
Smoked Trout Hash
with Scrambled Eggs

A neighborhood chef who can walk to the Brooklyn Borough Hall market from his restaurant, The Grocery, Charles Kiely is a familiar face at Greenmarket. You can see him chatting with farmers, sharing a cup of coffee, a doughnut, or a peach, depending on the season. This breakfast that Charlie made for me is fabulous and so simple—you can get the trout already smoked, and how hard is it to scramble eggs?

3 tablespoons olive oil
2 large shallots, sliced thin
4 small Carola potatoes, unpeeled ($3/4$ pound total), cut into $1/4$-inch dice
3 fresh sage leaves, chopped
12 ounces boneless smoked trout, skinned and cut into 1-inch pieces
Freshly ground pepper
4 large eggs
Kosher salt
1 tablespoon unsalted butter

Makes 2 servings

Heat 2 tablespoons of the oil in a medium nonstick skillet over medium heat. Add the shallots and cook, stirring, until tender, about 5 minutes. Add the potatoes and sage. Cook gently, stirring occasionally, until golden and tender, about 12 minutes.

Meanwhile, place the trout in a food processor and pulse to coarsely chop. Add to the skillet with the potatoes and sage. Season with pepper to taste. Cook until heated through; keep warm.

Lightly beat the eggs with salt and pepper to taste. In a small skillet over high heat, melt the butter with the remaining tablespoon of olive oil and cook the eggs, stirring, until scrambled as desired.

Divide the eggs between 2 plates and spoon the hash on top.

STACIE PIERCE

Strawberry-Rhubarb Compote

Stacie Pierce, formerly Union Square Cafe's pastry chef, has fond memories of summers spent on her mother's family farm in northern Michigan, which may be why she feels so much at home in the Union Square Greenmarket.

Her compote provides a perfect way to move from spring into early summer. It is delicious eaten by itself or as a topping for ice cream, yogurt, hot breakfast cereal, or buttered toast.

2	pints strawberries, cut in half
4	to 5 stalks rhubarb, trimmed and diced (3 $\frac{1}{2}$ to 4 cups)
$\frac{2}{3}$	cup sugar
$\frac{1}{2}$	teaspoon orange zest
$\frac{1}{2}$	cup fresh orange juice
1	tablespoon plus 1 teaspoon cornstarch
$\frac{1}{4}$	teaspoon freshly grated nutmeg
1	teaspoon fresh lemon juice

Makes 6 servings

In a saucepan over medium-low heat, combine half of the sliced strawberries with the rhubarb, sugar, orange zest, and $\frac{1}{4}$ cup of the orange juice. Simmer until the rhubarb is fork tender and the strawberries have lost some liquid, about 5 minutes.

In a small bowl, dissolve the cornstarch in the remaining orange juice.

Stir the cornstarch mixture into the warm fruit. Return the saucepan to medium-low heat and cook, stirring, about 2 minutes, until the mixture is clear. Remove from the heat and stir in the remaining strawberries, the lemon juice, and nutmeg. Pour into a bowl and let cool. May be refrigerated for up to 3 days.

CLAUDIA FLEMING
Poached Rhubarb with Goat Cheese Mascarpone

Claudia Fleming, pastry chef at Gramercy Tavern, shows us how to use rhubarb in its pure form, uninterrupted by other fruits. Here, she combines it with heavy cream, fresh mascarpone, and chévre from Greenmarket. All you need to complete the recipe will be a vanilla bean, orange peel, and a little Grand Marnier.

I suspect that many kids were frightened away from rhubarb, as I was, when my mother thought I was going to eat the leaves off my grandfather's rhubarb plants (the leaves can be toxic). I wasn't planning to, but she scared me anyway.

FOR THE POACHED RHUBARB
- 1 cup water
- 1 cup sugar
- 1/2 vanilla pod split, beans scraped out with a knife
- 1 pound (3 large stalks) rhubarb, trimmed and cut into 1/2-inch dice

Makes 6 servings

Combine the water and sugar in a medium saucepan and bring to a boil. Add the vanilla pod and beans and simmer for 10 minutes. Remove the pod.

Return the liquid to a boil. Add the diced rhubarb and simmer until just tender, about 5 minutes. With a slotted spoon, transfer the rhubarb from the liquid to an attractive serving bowl. Return the liquid to a simmer. Cook until reduced by two thirds, about 10 minutes. Set aside to cool slightly, then pour it over the rhubarb in the bowl. (You should have about 2 cups rhubarb in syrup.)

$^1/_2$ cup goat-milk yogurt ($3^1/_2$ ounces), or substitute cow's milk yogurt

1   cup mascarpone

1   cup heavy cream

$^2/_3$ cup crumbled and lightly packed chèvre (4 ounces)

3   tablespoons sugar

1   teaspoon finely grated orange zest

1   tablespoon Grand Marnier (optional)

In the bowl of an electric mixer, combine the yogurt, mascarpone, heavy cream, chèvre, and sugar. Using the whisk attachment, whip the mixture until stiff. Fold in the orange zest and Grand Marnier. (You should have about 5 cups.)

TO ASSEMBLE

Divide the goat cheese mascarpone among 6 goblets or saucer champagne glasses. Spoon the rhubarb on top.

BRIAN WOLF

Roasted Strawberry Clafouti

Brian Wolf, pastry chef at Michael's, makes pilgrimages to Greenmarkets around the city to get fresh fruit for the desserts that he makes at the restaurant. Here, he uses fresh strawberries, roasting them to concentrate the sugar and bring out their glorious flavor.

Clafouti is a French fruit dessert, midway between a cake and a pudding, most often made with cherries. This is not a dish that would normally be prepared outdoors, but Brian did just that one hot summer Saturday at one of our New York City Greenmarkets. You can make it at home, and top it with a dollop of whipped cream, crème fraîche, or mascarpone.

3	cups strawberries, rinsed, patted dry, and hulled
1/4	cup plus 1/3 cup sugar
6	large eggs
1/2	cup heavy cream
1	teaspoon vanilla extract
1/4	teaspoon salt
2/3	cup all-purpose flour
	Confectioners' sugar
	Whipped cream, crème fraîche, or mascarpone, optional, for serving

Makes 8 servings

Preheat the oven to 400°F. Lightly grease a jelly roll pan or half-sheet pan with sides. In a mixing bowl, toss together the strawberries and 1/4 cup of the sugar. Arrange the berries cut side down on the sheet and bake until soft to the touch, about 10 minutes. Set aside.

Lightly butter a 10½-inch fluted quiche dish. Set aside.

In a small bowl, whisk together the eggs, cream, vanilla, salt, and the remaining sugar. Sift the flour on top and stir just until blended; do not overmix.

Arrange the roasted strawberries in the prepared dish. Gradually pour the egg mixture on top.

Bake for 30 to 35 minutes until the batter is puffed and lightly golden. Let cool on a rack; it will shrink down as it cools. Dust with confectioners' sugar, cut into wedges, and serve warm or at room temperature.

STEPHANIE TEUWEN
Greenmarket Strawberry Sorbet

Stephanie Teuwen is a transplanted Frenchwoman working in the food industry who brought her love of farmers' markets and fresh fruit and vegetables to New York. Her approach to making fruity sorbet is easy and direct, and in this recipe, she makes it simple for all of us.

$\frac{1}{3}$	cup water
$\frac{2}{3}$	cup sugar
2	pints ripe strawberries, rinsed and hulled

Makes 4 servings

Bring the water and sugar to a boil in a saucepan over medium heat, stirring constantly. Remove from heat and let cool. (This makes 1 cup; it may be refrigerated up to 2 weeks.)

Puree the strawberries in a food processor. Stir in the syrup.

Transfer the mixture to an ice cream maker and freeze according to the manufacturer's instructions.

ANNE SALOMON
Herb Sorbet

Anne Salomon's Twee Fontein Herb Gardens stand at Greenmarket is the source for all things herbal, and Anne herself is an encyclopedia of information and lore. I enjoy no spring treat more than this one, Anne's fragrant, subtle sorbet made from her own organically grown fresh herbs.

2 cups water

3/4 cup sugar

1/2 cup fresh herbs or flowers, such as rose geranium, lemon verbena, antique rose petals with bitter white portion removed from bottom, or bee balm flower; or 1/4 cup rosemary leaves (1 large sprig) or fresh lavender flowers

1/2 cup fresh lemon juice

Makes 4 to 6 servings

Place the water and sugar in a medium saucepan over medium heat, and stir until the sugar is dissolved. Increase the heat and boil rapidly for 4 minutes. Remove from the heat, stir in the herbs, and let steep for 30 minutes. Strain, let cool, then stir in the lemon juice.

Transfer the mixture to an ice cream maker and freeze according to the manufacturer's instructions.

CONNIE McCABE
Rhubarb-Ginger Jam

Connie tells us: "I have always had a thing for rhubarb, going back to Grandma. I remember picking it out of her garden and eating it raw right on the spot. Years later, I came across this super-easy jam recipe, and I make heaps of it every spring. I am not a serious preserve maker, but this recipe has always worked for me."

2	pounds rhubarb (6 stalks), washed and cut into 1-inch pieces
2	cups sugar
One	3-ounce piece fresh ginger, peeled and cut into quarters

Makes 3 cups

Place the rhubarb, sugar, ginger, and about 1 cup water in a large saucepan over medium-low heat. Simmer, stirring occasionally and skimming the foam from the top, until the rhubarb is soft and a thick syrup has formed, about 20 minutes.

Remove the rhubarb with a slotted spoon and set aside. Simmer the syrup over medium-low heat until very thick, another 10 to 15 minutes, and remove from heat. Watch carefully so it does not caramelize. Remove and discard the ginger, and return the rhubarb to the pan.

Sterilize three 1-cup mason jars according to manufacturer's instructions. Transfer the jam to the hot, sterilized jars, tightly screw on the lids, and set aside at room temperature to set. The jam may be stored in the refrigerator for up to 6 months.

Appendix: Market Basket Edibles

Eggs

Chicken white, brown, and blue varieties.

Duck larger than chicken egg; cream, gray-blue, or
white shell, varies by breed; rich flavor.

Goose twice the size of chicken egg; off-white shell; very strong flavor.

Guinea Hen small; brown shell; rich, excellent flavor.

Pheasant one-third the size of chicken egg; brown, blue-green, or beige shell; light, delicate flavor.

Wild Turkey slightly larger than duck egg; beige shell with dark-brown speckles; balanced, full flavored.

Fish and Seafood

Cod sweet, delicate flavor, lean flesh; use cooked.

Bass, Sea lean, white, moderately firm, bony, delicate sweet flesh.

Bass, Striped lean, firm, snow-white flesh.

Blackfish lean, firm white flesh; delicate sweet flavor; skin may have a bitter taste.

Bluefish distinctly flavored, oily, dark flesh.

Butterfish small; silvery skin; very sweet flesh.

Clams meaty texture; distinct flavor.

Crab tender, sweet-flavored flesh.

Flounder, Black-Backed excellent, mild flavor; tender, white flesh.

Flounder, Yellow Tail sweet flavor, thinner than summer flounder; use cooked.

Fluke (Summer Flounder) mild sweet flavor.

Lobster tender, luscious flesh.

Oysters refreshing, sweet briny taste.

Mackerel, Boston high fat content; sweet, very rich flavor.

Mackerel, Spanish rich flavor, milder than other mackerels; dark flesh.

Monkfish firm, very lean, mild white flesh.

Scrod (Hake) bland flavor, soft texture; fishmongers may interchange whiting, hake, or smaller members of the cod family; use cooked.

Sea Scallops ivory white to pinkish-orange, succulent flesh; use cooked.

Shad a bony relative of the herring, rich-tasting. Shad roe is even more popular than the fish itself.

Skate lean, mild flavor.

Sole, Gray (Flounder) white, firm flesh; delicate, mildly sweet flavor.

Squid neutral tasting, takes on the flavor of what it is cooked with.

Trout, Freshwater off-white to salmon-pink flesh, firm texture, rich flavor.

Trout, Sea (Weakfish) delicate, sweet flavor.

Whelk (Conch) meaty, clamlike taste and texture; sold in or out of the shell.

Whiting related to cod and hake; white, very sweet mild flavor.

Flowers, Edible

Borage cool blue blossoms. See also Herb Chart, page 173.

Chive Blossom resembles large clover blossom.

Cilantro Flower whitish-lavender flower, resembles Queen Anne's Lace; mild, spicy flavor.

Dianthus (Carnation, Pink) sweet and lovely.

Gem Marigold delicate, little flower; yellow, tangerine colors.

Johnny-Jump-Up larger, creamy, yellow-white version of Viola; mild flavor.

Lavender tall, fragrant blossoms; colors include cloud white, powder blue, deep purple, and lavender.

Nasturtium brightly painted blossoms, gold, mahogany, orange, purple, blue, yellow; sparkly hot flavor.

Rose fragrant and sweet; always cut the rose at its base to avoid the bitter-tasting white bottom.

Rosemary Flowers deep-purple, tiny blossoms; intense flavor.

Sage (Honey Melon, Pineapple) both are fruity and nectar filled.

Viola tender, pinky-nail size; deep purple with reddish-gold dot in the center; mild flavor.

Zucchini Blossom long, narrow, soft orange flowers; mild fragrance and taste.

Fruit

Apricot heart-shaped, velvety, beautifully colored skin and flesh; pastel blends of oranges, yellows and pinks; firm, juicy flesh; tropical aromas; use raw or cooked.

Apples See Apple Chart, page 79.

Blueberry (Highbush) plump, round shape; bluish-black, bloomy skin; mild, sweet-tart flavor; use raw or cooked.

Blueberry (Lowbush), Wild Blueberry small fruit, more intense flavor; use raw or cooked.

Blackberry tight, black, hollow helmets; tart and sweet balance; use raw or cooked.

Cherry, Sweet red, yellow, purple, bluish, or white skin; textures from firm and crisp to soft and juicy; slightly tart to winy sweet flavor; use raw or cooked. **Sour (Pie)** dull pinkish-red, yellow, bright red, red-black, or mahogany skin; slightly acidic to bittersweet, astringent flavors; use raw or cooked.

Cranberry irregular-marble-shaped, crimson-red, tart-sweet flesh; use raw, cooked, in juice.

Currant small BB-size fruit, sold in clusters; juicy, firm flesh; use raw or cooked. **Red** mildly acidic, low sugar. **Black** subtle, foxy aroma; medium sugar. **White** low acid, rich sugary flavor.

Elderberry shiny blue-black clusters of tiny, round fruit; tart, bitter flavor; may be eaten raw, but best cooked.

Gooseberry translucent, fat, lime-green to soft-purple ovals; firm, juicy tart flesh; may be eaten raw, but usually cooked.

Grapes, Seedless all used raw or cooked. *Canadice* bright red skin, fragrant, sweet, mild, winy flavor. *Einset* bright red skin, thin waxy bloom, crisp, juicy flesh with hints of strawberries. *Himrod* greenish-yellow skin and flesh, juicy, bright flavor. *Vanessa* deep-red; oval shape; crisp, juicy flesh; very sweet and fragrant.

Grapes, Seeded all used raw or cooked *Caco* light red fruit; juicy flesh; aromatic, rich, sweet flavor. *Catawba* reddish-purple; luscious, slightly foxy

flavor. *Concord* black-skin; juicy flesh; balance sweet with tart, foxy aftertaste. *Diamond* greenish-yellow skin and flesh, bright-sweet flavor, excellent for juice. *Niagara* white version of Concord, juicy, foxy sweet.

Melon *Cantaloupe* round, mostly rough skinned, but not netted; grayish-green to white-green skin; thick, sweet, deep-orange, aromatic flesh. Popular varieties are Savor and Charantais. *Muskmelon* heavily netted or webbed skin, often sold as cantaloupe; rich flavor; very aromatic, creamy flesh that can be green, salmon-pink, or yellow depending on the variety. Popular varieties are Galia, Jenny Lind, Green Fleshed, Harvest Queen, Sierra Gold, Salmon-Pink Fleshed, Sharlyn, White Fleshed. *Watermelon* round to oblong cylindrical shape; 2 pounds to over 100 pounds; smooth dark-green to dull-green

rind with overlaid darker stripes; moderately textured, crisp, red, yellow, and orange flesh; very sweet and juicy; seeded and seedless varieties. Popular Red varieties are Black Diamond, Moon and Stars, Sugar Baby; Yellow varieties are Yellow Baby, Orangelo.

Mulberry long, conical, shaped fruit; purple or white skin and flesh; creamy texture; very aromatic, sweet, juicy; use raw or cooked.

Nectarine oval shape; smooth, white or yellow skin; white varieties are often blushed with red or purple, yellow varieties with dark-red or scarlet; firm, very juicy flesh; essence of apricots, peaches, and almonds; use raw or cooked.

Peach, Freestone the flesh separates easily from the pit; use raw or cooked. *Halehaven* medium-size, round, dark-red skin, yellow flesh; rich flavor, melt-in-your-mouth texture. *Jersey Queen* large, oval fruit; yellow skin with dark red blush; firm, mildly sweet flesh; use raw or cooked. *Stark Saturn (Flat or Doughnut Peach)* flattened oval shape; pastel-yellow skin blushed with red, white flesh; sweet, tender, melting quality; best raw. *Iron Mountain* creamy-white skin with pale green overtones, white flesh; juicy, sweet, late season; use raw or cooked.

Peach, Cling flesh sticks to the pit; early season; seldom available at farmers' markets; used mainly for commercial canning.

Pears, Asian use raw or cooked. *Kosui (Good Water)* medium-size, slightly russeted golden-bronze skin; crisp, white flesh; sweet and juicy, mellow flavor with hints of grass and vanilla. *Seuri* large, rounded oval; greenish-brown skin with some yellow-orange russeting; white fine-grain, sweet, aromatic flesh. *Shinseiki (New Century)* medium to large, rounded oval; smooth, thick yellow skin; sweet, mild flavor; crisp, tender, juicy.

Pears, Western *Clapp's Favorite (Red Clapp's Favorite)* medium to large, pastel lemon-yellow skin; juicy, sweet, yellow flesh. *Bartlett* medium-size, classic pear shape, pale green; becomes golden yellow when fully ripe; juicy, white flesh; sweet, slightly tart flavor; highly perfumed. Red Bartletts have a finer grain and higher sugar level than pale varieties. *Bosc* large, tapered neck; dark-yellow skin with brown russet finish, yellowish-white, finely-grained flesh; exotic nutty-vanilla flavors. *Devoe* medium-size; slender green-skinned or red blushed skin; ivory-white, finely grained flesh; pear flavor. *Seckle* small size; green undertones with brown-russet overlay; rich, sweet taste.

Plum squat, oval, heart-shaped, and marble shapes; marble- to tennis-ball size; golden-yellow, lemony-green, black-purple skins, almost all with a natural bloom (dusty, filmy-white coating). *President* large, oval, dark-purple skin, tinged with black, yellow, dry flesh; savory, rich plum flavor. *Blue Damson* small, oval; blue-black skin; firm, greenish-yellow flesh; tart and juicy flavor. *Green Gage* yellowish-green; medium rounded ovals; green-yellow flesh; mild, sweet flavor with tart overtones. *Mirabelle* small oval, slightly tapered at the top; muted, golden-yellow skin with occasional brown speckles; light yellow, crisp flesh; delicate, sweet flavor. *Prune (Imperial Epineuse, Italian, Stanley)* large oval; purple-red, purple-black, deep-blue, greenish-yellow flesh; juicy, aromatic, richly flavored. *Shiro* Japanese type; medium-size, Ping-Pong ball shaped; transparent, soft-yellow skin; juicy, sweet, tender flesh. *Elephant Heart* Japanese type; large, heart-shaped fruit, thick brownish-purple skin; juicy, blood-red, full-flavored, sweet flesh. *Methley* Japanese type; small, round fruit; purple skin with splashes of red; very juicy, sweet, creamy flesh.

Quince round apple-pear shape; bright-green, fuzzy skin; dense, creamy-white flesh; vanilla-citrus flavor and fragrance; usually cooked.

Raspberry penny-size, hollow, oval fruit; seeded, larger varieties resemble thimbles; firm but tender flesh; flavor ranges from tart to sweet; use raw or cooked. *Black* large, glossy-black fruit, low acid, good sugar. *Purple* deep-purple, pastel skin and flesh, fragrant and sweet. *Red* dull, pinkish-red to brilliant, glossy-red skin and flesh; fragrant, balance of tart and sweet. *Yellow* bright yellow to orange-gold-colored skin and flesh; juicy, excellent flavor.

Strawberry bright pink to crimson-red, blocky heart shape; highly aromatic, acidic and tart to intensely sweet, firm flesh; use raw or cooked.

Greens, Salad and Cooking

Amaranth tender, broad, green leaves with red-stained centers; flavor reminiscent of artichokes and spinach; use raw or cooked.

Amaranth, Red small, pointy leaves; mild, sweet flavor; use raw.

Arugula dark-green oak-leaf-shaped leaves; spicy, nutty flavor; use raw or cooked.

Bok Choy large, white-green barrel shaped; mildly sweet, crisp, moist leaves; use raw or cooked.

Broccoli Rabe (Rapini) dark-green, leafy stalks with clusters of small, broccoli-like buds; warm, slightly bitter flavor; sauté or steam.

Collards soft blue-green, crumpled, tattered leaves on long stems; rich, green flavor.

Cress, Pepper tiny leaves; peppery but not hot flavor; use raw.

Cress, Upland large leaves; milder than watercress; use raw or cooked.

Curly Endive (Frisée) dark-green, leaf-lettuce-type head or frilly crisp leaves; pleasing, mild, bitter taste; use in salads when young.

Dandelion, Baby long, pointy, green leaves; nutty, slightly bitter; use raw or lightly cooked.

Dandelion, Red or Green larger, jagged-edged leaves; more pronounced nutty-bitter flavor; use raw or cooked.

Escarole greenish-white leafy heads, crisp texture, slightly bitter; use raw or cooked.

Fennel, Bronze brownish-purple, feathery leaves; delicate anise flavor; use raw or cooked.

Kale, Baby often sold as Red Russian or Blue Siberian Kale; curly, ragged-edged leaves; tender texture, sweet flavor; use raw or cooked.

Lamb's Quarters dusty-green leaves; grassy, spinachlike flavor; use raw or cooked.

Lettuce *Baby Lettuce, Mixed* tender leaves of young lettuce; use raw. *Mesclun* mixture of tender, young lettuce, herbs, and edible flowers that varies from grower to grower (see page 36).

Mâche (Corn Salad) light-green leaf clusters; delicate, buttery flavor; use raw.

Miner's Lettuce pale-green, fat, cloverlike leaves; juicy, mild mineral taste; use raw.

Mibuna clumpy head of long narrow, green leaves with rounded tips; strong, distinct mibuna flavor; use raw or cooked.

Microgreens pea shoots, delicate $1/4$-inch leaves of radish, broccoli, and other vegetables; refreshing, concentrated, green-sweet flavors; use raw.

Mizuna glossy, green feathery leaves; warm, nutty flavor; use raw.

Mustard large, green leaves, purpled-tinged curly ends; spicy, full flavored; use cooked.

Mustard, Baby small red, green-tinged leaves; warm, zippy flavor; use raw.

Mustard, Red large, green leaves, purple tinged curly ends; spicy, full flavored; use raw or cooked.

Pac Choi, Baby 4- to 6-inch vase-shaped heads; green, tender, spoon-shaped leaves; crisp and sweet; use cooked.

Purslane juicy, refreshing, mild-mineral flavor; use raw.

Radicchio tight heads of red to green, white-tinged leaves; some types are open headed, similar to romaine lettuce; watery, crunchy, with mildly bitter taste; use raw or cooked.

Red Orach (Mountain Spinach) soft-magenta to crimson-red leaves; mild, spinachlike flavor; use raw or cooked.

Shungiku (Edible Chrysanthemum) soft-green serrated leaves; warm, tangy herbaceous flavor; use raw or cooked.

Sorrel bright-green, smooth, arrow-shaped leaves; grassy, lemony taste; use for salad, soups, sauces.

Spinach dark-green, crinkled leaves; juicy, mildly acidic taste; use young leaves raw, cook larger leaves.

Sprouts, Radish, Broccoli, Onion, Sunflower, Daikon, Buckwheat slim, crisp shoots; delicate flavor, some with hints of spice or sweetness; use raw or cooked.

Swiss Chard long, narrow stems with crinkly red, pink, yellow, and green arrow-shaped leaves; stems have delicate, celery flavor; leaves have rich, mineral flavor; use raw or cooked.

Watercress, Wild green leaves; steamy, spicy, nutty flavor; use raw or cooked.

Herbs

See Herb Chart, page 173.

Mushrooms, Cultivated

Button off-white, size varies; firm texture, mild flavor; use raw or cooked.

Cremini light brown version of button; firm flesh, full flavored; use raw or cooked.

Portobello large, fully developed cremini; dark-brown, flat 3- to 6-inch caps; meaty taste and texture; use cooked.

Shiitake small to medium-size caps, tanned brown leather finish; full, mildly sweet flavor; use cooked.

Mushrooms, Wild

Amethyst Deceiver upturned, small, lilac-colored caps, leggy stems; delicate flavor; use cooked.

Blewit medium-round, somewhat stout, bright lilac caps and stems; delicate, bright flavors; use raw or cooked.

Chanterelle golden-apricot-colored little trumpets; dry texture, mild earthy flavor; use cooked.

Hedgehog (Pied de Mouton) "poor man's lobster"; flat, cream-colored, ruffled, pointy, open caps; spongy, medium-firm texture; sweet, luscious flesh; use cooked.

Hen of the Woods resembles gray-white clump of ruffled hen's feathers; spongy, stringy texture; wild, smoky, woody flavor; use cooked.

Honey creamy-yellow, long-stemmed clusters; firm,

slightly slimy texture; delicate earthy flavor; use cooked.

Horse Mushroom (Field) large, wild version of button; rich flavor, hints of anise, mossy fragrance; use raw or cooked.

Morel deep brown, spongelike cones; firm flesh, rich flavor; use cooked.

Oyster (Tree Mushroom, *Hiratake*) dull, dusty-gray, leafy fan shape; rich, savory flavor; may be eaten raw but flavor mellows when cooked.

Porcini (Cèpe) broad, brown cap over stubby, white stem; savory, rich flavor; use cooked.

Puffball large, milk-white to chocolate-brown color, roundish shape; sweet, refined mushroom flavor; use cooked.

Nuts

Black Walnut buttery texture and earthy, smoky, butterlike flavor; use raw or cooked.

Butternut (White Walnut) milder, less meaty version of Black Walnut; hints of anise.

Peppers

See also Pepper Chart, page 33.

Bell red, yellow, green, lavender, chocolate colors; sweet and aromatic; use raw or cooked.

Frying red, pale green, elongated shape; sweet to medium hot; use raw or cooked.

Hot all colors of the rainbow; wide range of shapes and sizes; aromatic, fruity flavors; warm to explosive heat; use raw, cooked, or dried.

Spice bell-like shape; sweet flavor, medium heat; use raw, cooked, or dried, as in paprika.

Poultry, Meat, and Game

(Birds can be raised year-round, but small growers tend to follow traditional bird and hunter cycles, harvesting in fall and winter.)

Boar, Wild moist, lean sweet flesh; intense pork flavor with hints of red meat.

Capon large meaty, very tender, moist flesh; savory flavor.

Chicken tender, juicy, lean; light flavor.

Cornish Game Hen small; butterlike texture; very sweet flavor.

Duck, Muscovy large, meaty; dark moist flesh; rich flavor.

Duck, Pekin pinker, paler flesh than Muscovy; slightly milder flavor.

Goose dense dark flesh; beefy flavor.

Guinea Hen meat is darker in September; tender, rich tasting.

Partridge similar to pheasant; sweeter, milder flavor.

Pheasant, Soup delicate white to pale-pink flesh, more fatty than younger birds; sweet mild flavor.

Pheasant (Young) white to pale-pink flesh, firm texture; delicate, sweet, mild flavor.

Quail juicy, tender flesh; delicate flavor.

Rabbit tender, succulent flesh; sweet, very mild flavor.

Turkey, Domestic larger than farm-raised wild turkey; mild flavor.

Turkey, Wild, Farm Raised smaller than domestic turkey, lean flesh; rich gamy flavor.

Venison finely grained flesh; very rich flavor.

Root Crops

Beet use all types raw or cooked. *Golden* Ping-Pong ball to baseball size; fruity, mild flavor. *Red* golf-ball to softball size; sweet, sugary flavor. *Formosa* long, cylindrical shape; sweet red flesh. *Striped (Chioggia, or Candy Cane)* Italian heirloom; Ping-Pong ball to tennis-ball size; pinkish-red skin with pink-red striped white flesh. *White* golf-ball to baseball size; mild, sweet flavor.

Burdock *(Gobo)* brown, hairy, tapered body; strong, sweet, earthy flavor; use raw when very young, cook older roots.

Carrot various shapes and sizes; colors include orange, white, red, and yellow.

Celeriac large, knobby, brown-skinned root with celerylike stalks and leaves; firm, crisp flesh; nutty-sweet, mild flavor; use raw or cooked.

Cilantro Root small, tapered root of cilantro (see also Herb Chart, page 173); pungent, use cooked.

Daikon long, tapered, or short, rounded varieties; crisp texture, mild flavor; use raw or cooked.

Garlic (Rocambole or Top-Setting Varieties) more flavor than standard types, no bitterness; use raw or cooked.

Garlic Top edible green bud of top-setting garlic; white, feathery flower inside; mild garlic taste; use raw or cooked. Cook older, dried tops.

Ginseng small, pale-brown-skinned root, somewhat human-shaped; use raw or cooked.

Horseradish knobby shape, pale-brown skin over white flesh; extremely hot, pungent flavor; use raw.

Jerusalem Artichoke (Sunchoke) brown-skinned, small, irregular-shaped knobs; mild, nutty flavor; refreshing crunch of water chestnuts; use raw or slightly cooked.

Kohlrabi (Cabbage Turnip) odd-looking, smooth-skinned, pale-green or milky purple palm-sized globes; widely spaced, broccoli-like leaves growing out of the sides; nutty-sweet taste; use raw or cooked.

Leek fat, white, scallion-type base with wide green leaves on top; sweet, subtle onion flavor; use cooked.

Onion, Bunching (Spring Onion) immature, undeveloped onion; pleasing, sweet flavor; use raw or cooked.

Onion, Fresh or Sandwich (Young onions that have yet to form a tight, papery outer skin. They tend to be sweeter and are particularly good for eating raw.) *Red Torpedo* spindle-shaped; light-purple flesh; sweet, mildly pungent flavor. *White Bermuda* large, partially flattened, crisp texture, mild flavor. *Sweet Flat Red* large, flattened; red skin, white flesh with red rings; very mild taste. *Walla Walla* big, flattened globe; light-brown skin, extremely mild, sweet flavor; similar to Vidalia, Maui.

Onion, Storage or Keeper *Cippolini* flattened spheres, papery skin, purplish-red or white skin and flesh. *Ailsa Craig* large, up to 2 pounds; globe-shaped, Spanish type; papery skin; sweet, firm mild flesh.

Parsley Root beige skin, carrot shape, smaller than parsnip; delicate, mild flavor; use cooked.

Parsnip beige skin, oversize-carrot shape; earthy taste.

Potato see Potato Chart, page 137.

Radish use raw or cooked. *Black* round, black, rough-skinned tennis ball and larger size; crisp texture; pungent, almost hot flavor; use raw or cooked. *China Rose* blunt-shaped version of Daikon; bright, rose-colored skin; crisp, sharp-white flesh; very pungent flavor. *Daikon* long, tapered or short, rounded varieties; crisp texture; mild flavor. *French Breakfast* rose-colored shoulders, blunt, white bottoms; tender, crisp; mildly pungent.

Ramp (Wild Leek) looks like a cross between lily of the valley and scallion with a round bulb bottom and a little root, a white to red stalk, and deep-green leaves that fan out on top; pungent, earthy, garlic flavor; use raw or cooked.

Rutabaga softball size; purple-pale-orange waxy skin; dense, moist, sweet, flavorful orange-yellow flesh; use cooked.

Salsify (Oyster Plant) brown skin; narrow, carrot shape; delicate-tasting white flesh, hints of oyster; use cooked.

Scallion slender, white-based member of the onion family with hollow green leaves; milder than spring onion; use raw or cooked.

Shallot resembles garlic cloves; pink-red papery skin; subtle onion flavor; used raw or cooked.

Sweet Potato knobby, irregularly shaped tubers; yellowish-orange to white flesh; moister varieties, sometimes called Louisiana Yams, are most flavorful and richer tasting; use cooked.

Turnip milk-white to purplish-white skin; tennis-ball or smaller size is best; nutty delicate flavor; use cooked, young leaves are also cooked.

Tomatoes

See also Tomato Chart, page 28. Use raw or cooked.

Beefsteak large, palm-size fruit.

Cherry (includes pear shaped) fat, cherry-size fruit; concentrated flavor.

Currant clusters of grape-size fruit; aromatic, winy, intense flavors.

Husk (Cape Gooseberry, Poha, Ground Cherry) not tomatoes but invariably displayed next to the tomatoes; marble-size fruit; green when immature, golden-yellow when ripe; always wrapped in a papery membrane (husk). The immature have tangy, citrus flavor; ripe have fruity, pineapple flavor.

Plum egg-shaped, thick-fleshed, meaty fruit; not too juicy.

Tomatillo (larger cousin of Husk) green or purple flesh when immature, golden-yellow when ripe; tangy, herbaceous flavor.

Vegetables

Asparagus green, purple-tinged stalks with fine, paint-brush-like tips; unique rich flavor; use raw or cooked.

Beans, Dried all have earthy, nutty flavors; toothsome, creamy textures; use cooked. *Cranberry* small, rounded; tan undercoat, specks and streaks of pinkish-burgundy. *Great Northern* small, white kidney shape. *Jacob's Cattle* shiny white, speckled with deep maroon. *Navy* small white ovals. *Pinto* small tan ovals covered with brownish-red specks. *Red Kidney* large, brownish-red, kidney shape. *Black Turtle* deep, chocolate color.

Beans, Fresh (Shelling) *Cranberry* soft-green pods copiously splashed with pinkish red; use cooked. *Fava (Broad Bean)* 4 to 8 inches long; filmy, light-green rounded pods; meaty texture, full flavor; use cooked (remove skin). *Lima* dull green, curved, flat pods; buttery taste and texture; use cooked. *Soy (Edamame)* 2 to 3 inches, curved, bumpy, dull-green pods; buttery, nutlike taste; use cooked.

Beans, Snap (String, Pole, Bush) "snap" when broken; many colors. *Yellow Wax, Burgundy, Green and Yellow varieties* use raw or cooked. *French Filet (Haricot Vert)* the young, tender pickings of the above varieties.

Brussels Sprouts quarter-size, green or red cabbage heads; sweet, nutty cabbage flavor; use cooked.

Bitter Melon 8-inch-long tapered fruits; dull-green, highly warted, waxy alligator-like skin; white flesh;

bitter flavor with hints of okra and eggplant; use cooked.

Cabbage Cabbage (Red and Green types) large round heads; some varieties may be more flat than round; 3 1/2 pounds to over 20 pounds; bland or rich, sweet-earthy flavor; use raw or cooked.

Cabbage, Savoy loose heads of highly crinkled leaves; green has a delicious buttery taste and texture; use raw or cooked.

Cauliflower all types may be used cooked or raw. *White* shaped like domed sea coral; crisp texture; mild, buttery flavor. *Broccoflower (Cauli-Broc)* broccoli-green color; domed heads; milder and sweeter than cauliflower. *Romanesco Broccoli* small, pointed, spiral-shaped heads; bright lime-green color; distinct, rich flavor. *Purple* similar to white; loses color when cooked.

Celery compact, dark-green or red bunches of upright stalks; crunchy, moist, refreshing mineral flavor; use raw or cooked.

Corn *Bi-Color (Yellow and White) Butter and Sugar, Peaches, Twice-as-Nice. White* Howling Mob, How Sweet It Is, Silver Queen. *Yellow* Jubilee.

Cucumber *Aria* dark-green Middle-Eastern variety; 4 to 8 inches long; sweet; use raw. *Lemon* slicing variety; short, oval shape; thin white skin; hint of lemon flavor; use raw. *Jersey Pickle* Kirby style, short, stubby, spiny, light green-white skin; mild flavor; use raw or pickled. *Suyo Long* deep-green; oriental variety; narrow spiny body, about 1 foot long; "burpless," few seeds, crisp texture, excellent

flavor; use raw or pickled.

Eggplant *Bambino* 2-inch glossy, black ovals; a little bitter; use cooked. *Kermit (Thai)* 2- to 3-inch squat ovals; shades of light- and dark-green with splashes of white; meaty, pungent flesh; use cooked. *Rosa Bianca* unevenly shaped; lavender and creamy-white skin; palm-size globes; sweet, meaty, creamy-white flesh; use cooked. *Turkish Orange* 3-inch, bright-orange-red-skinned spheres; sweet but somewhat seedy flesh; may be eaten when somewhat green; use cooked.

Fennel whitish-green, flat, celerylike bulb with slightly ribbed green stalks; feathery, frilly leaves; crisp and crunchy; warm anise aroma and flavor; used cooked or raw.

Fiddlehead Fern (Ostrich Fern) dull-green, tightly coiled fern top (resembles the curved top of a fiddle); chewy texture, green bean-asparagus flavor; use cooked.

Okra blond-green to ruby red, depending on variety; 5-sided, finger-size tapered pods; mild flavor; best when under 4 inches long and firm; use cooked or raw.

Pea, English (Shelling or Green Pea) green, fat, nonedible pod; sweet, crunchy; use raw or lightly cooked.

Pea, Snow wafer-thin, bright-green, translucent, edible pods; sweet and tender; use raw or cooked.

Pea, Sugar Snap (Sugar Pea) plump, bright-green, edible pods; crisp and sweet; "snap" when broken open; use raw or lightly cooked.

Pumpkin see Squash Chart, page 134.

Rhubarb pinkish-cherry-colored stalks (leaves are not edible); tart taste, hints of sweet and sour; use cooked.

Squash, Summer *Scallop (Pattypan, Sunburst)* green, yellow, dull-white flattened disks; some more scalloped than others; fine-grained, sweet, moist flesh; use raw or cooked. *Zucchini: Cocozelle (Marrow)* long, narrow, ribbed; dark-green stripes on greenish-yellow skin; flavorful, firm, white flesh; best under 8 inches; use raw or cooked. *Cucuzzi (Bottle Gourd; Long Green)* pale-green, shiny, thick skin; $1^1/2$ to 3 feet long; twisted, buglelike gourd; very firm, sweet white flesh; used peeled and cooked. *Lita (Lebanese)* dull, lime-green, lightbulb-shaped; creamy, well-flavored flesh; use raw or cooked. *Ronde de Nice* round, 5 to 8 inches across; pale-green skin, creamy-white, richly flavored flesh; use raw or cooked. *Tenerumi (Squash Runners)* young tendril-like shoots of the cucuzzi; use cooked. *Yellow Crookneck* deep-yellow warty skin; thin neck, bent over its bulbous bottom; mild, pale-yellow flesh; use raw or cooked.

Squash, Winter see Squash Chart, page 134. *Butternut* bulbous shape; thick tan skin; sweet, mild-flavored flesh; use cooked.

Resource Guide

Every day of the year there is a greenmarket or farmers' market open for business somewhere in America. In the heart of New York City, Hilo, Hawaii, New Orleans, Louisiana, or San Francisco, California, farmers gather to sell the fruits and vegetables of their labors.

What follows is a list of some popular markets. Days and hours of operation may change seasonally, so call ahead to obtain schedules. If your local market is not included here, call your Chamber of Commerce, City Hall, or Department of Consumer Affairs for information. And if your town or city doesn't have a greenmarket, start one!

Farmers' Market Resource List

California

Berkeley Farmers Market
Center Street & Martin Luther King
    Boulevard
Berkeley, CA
Year-round—Saturday
Contact: Kirk Lumpkin
(510) 548-3333

Davis Farmers Market
4th & C Streets in Central Park
Davis, CA
Year-round—Wednesday & Saturday
Contact: Randii MacNear
(530) 756-1695

Healdsburg Farmers Market
North & Vine Streets
Healdsburg, CA
Seasonal—Tuesday & Saturday
Contact: Renee Kiff
(707) 431-1956

San Francisco Alemany Farmers Market
100 Alemany Boulevard
San Francisco, CA
Seasonal—Saturday
Contact: Karol Kappel
(415) 647-9423

San Francisco Ferry Plaza Farmers Market
San Francisco, CA
Embarcadero & Green Streets
—Saturdays
Market & Embarcadero at
Justin Herman Plaza—Tuesdays
Year-round
Contact: Sibella Kraus
(415) 981-3004

Santa Monica Farmers' Market
Santa Monica, CA
Arizona Avenue at the 3rd Street
Promenade
Year-round—Wednesday & Saturday
Contact: Laura Avery
(310) 458-8712

District of Columbia

Freshfarm Market
20th Street at Dupont Circle
Washington, DC
Seasonal—Sunday
Contact: Ann Harvey Yonkers
(202) 331-7300

Georgia

Morningside Farmers' Market
1325 North Highland Avenue (parking
lot of Indigo Costal Grill)
Atlanta, GA
Seasonal—Saturday
Contact: Roxanne Hay
(770) 788-8707

Hawaii

Hilo Farmers Market
Corner of Mamo Street & Kamehameha
Avenue
Hilo, HI
Year-round—Wednesday & Saturday
Contact: Keith De La Cruz
(808) 933-1000

Illinois

Chicago's Green City Market
Near North
Chicago, IL
Seasonal—Weekdays
Contact: Abby Mandel
(847) 835-2240

Iowa

Washington Farmers' Market
№1 Downtown Square in Central Park
Seasonal—Thursday
№2 Orscheln-Pamida-U.S.D.A.
Parking Lot
Seasonal—Sunday
Washington, IA
Contact: Bob Shepherd
(319) 653-4888

Louisiana

Crescent City Farmers Market
700 Magazine Street
New Orleans, LA
Year-round—Saturday
Contact: Richard McCarthy
(504) 861-5898

Maine

Camden Farmers Market
Colcord Street
Camden, ME
Seasonal—Wednesday & Saturday
Contact: John Barnstein
(207) 273-2809

Maryland

Saint Michael's Freshfarm Market
Muskrat Park
Saint Michael's, MD
Seasonal—Saturday
Contact: Ann Harvey Yonkers
(202) 331-7300

Takoma Park Farmers Market
Old Town on Laurel Avenue
Takoma Park, MD
Seasonal—Sunday
Contact: Francis Roland
(301) 270-1700, ext. 205

Massachusetts

Newton Farmer's Market
Cold Spring Park at Beacon Street
Newton Highlands, MA
Seasonal—Tuesday
Contact: Judy Dore
(617) 552-7120

Northampton Farmers' Market
Gothic Street, Downtown
Northampton, MA
Seasonal—Saturday
Contact: Cynthia Tobin
(413) 527-3603

Waltham Farmers' Market
Main & Moody Streets
Waltham, MA
Seasonal—Saturday
Contact: Jennifer Rose
(781) 893-0361

Montana

Missoula Farmers Market
Circle Square & Higgins Avenue
Missoula, MT
Seasonal—Tuesday & Saturday
Contact: Mel Parker
(406) 777-2636

New Mexico

Santa Fe Farmers Market
Santa Fe Rail Yard
Santa Fe, NM
Seasonal—Tuesday, Saturday &
   Sunday
Contact: Pamela Roy
(505) 983-4098

New York

Greenmarket
Union Square Park (East 17th Street
   & Broadway)
Year-round—Monday, Wednesday,
   Friday & Saturday
Contact: Joel Patraker
(212) 477-3220

North Carolina

**Greensboro Farmers' Curb
   Market**
501 Yanceyville Street
Greensboro, NC
Year-round—Tuesday, Thursday &
   Saturday
Contact: Larry Smith
(336) 373-2402

Ohio

Oberlin Farmers' Market
South Main Street; Route 58 across
   from McDonald's
Oberlin, OH
Seasonal—Tuesday & Saturday
Contact: Ken Sloane
(440) 775-4158

Texas

**Austin's Historic Farmers'
   Market**
6701 Burnet Road
Austin, TX
Year-round—Daily
Contact: Hill Rylander
(512) 454-1002

San Antonio Farmers Market
Olmos Basin on Jackson-Keller Street
San Antonio, TX
Seasonal—Tuesday & Saturday
Contact: Ms. Margo
(210) 820-0288

Vermont

Newport Farmers Market
Causeway at Gardener Park
Newport, VT
Seasonal—Wednesday & Saturday
Contact: JoAnn Martin
(802) 754-8405

Stowe Farmers Market
Route 108 at Red Barn Shop
Stowe, VT
Seasonal—Sunday
Contact: Elizabeth Squier
(802) 253-8532

Virginia

**Arlington County Farmers'
  Market**
North 14th Street & North Courthouse
Arlington, VA
Seasonal—Saturday
Contact: Tom Tyler
(703) 228-6423

Washington

Bellingham Farmers' Market
№1 Railroad & Chestnut Avenues
Seasonal—Saturday & Sunday

№ 2 Old Fairhaven Village
Seasonal—Wednesday
Bellingham, WA
Contact: Karen Durham
(360) 647-2060

**University District Farmers
  Market**
Northeast 50th Street & University Way
  NE
Seattle, WA
Seasonal—Saturday
Contact: Chris Curtis
(206) 547-2278

Wisconsin

**Dane County Farmers'
  Market**
Capitol Square
Madison, WI
Seasonal—Wednesday & Saturday
Contact: Mary Carpenter
(920) 563-5037

Index

Captions

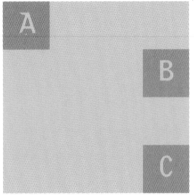

Page 12

A—Lucus at the Locust Grove stand
B—Don Keller
C—The Cantors

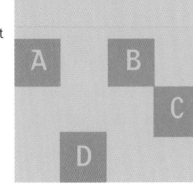

Page 74

A—Bob Messerich of Knoll Krest Farm
B—Ron Bianghi, Jr., of Stokes Farm
C—Stephanie Villani
D—Greenmarket's Field Supervisor Brendan Corr

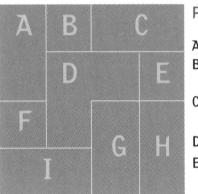

Page 17

A—Simon Glenn-Gregg
B—Noni and Walter Bauer
C—Bill McGraw Gray of Rockhill Bakehouse
D—Don Keller
E—Greenmarket staffer Lynn Peemoeler
F—Hong-Antran, Greenmarket staffer
G—Faye Chan of the Fifth Floor Kitchen
H—Mike at the Locust Grove stand
I—Gray Kunz, Joel Patraker, and Tim Stark

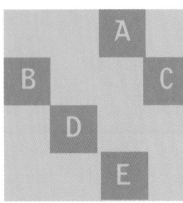

Page 130

A—David, Eric, and Ted from Oak Grove Plantation
B—Jim Grillo
C—Howard Cantor
D—Jack Gunn
E—Arthur Schwartz and Iris Caralli

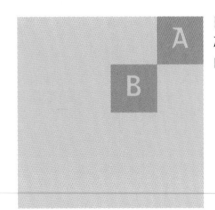

Page 22
A—Renis Garner
B—Keith Stewart

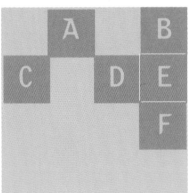

Page 168
A—Rick Bishop and Tamara Holt
B—Bernadette Kowalski
C—Joe Cuniglio, Greenmarket manager
D—Lloyd Feit of Cafe Loup
E—Suzi Dare of Cherry Lane Farms
F—Author with Uncle Sidney Thomas

Eggplants
Melon from Ted Bleu
Peaches } Mr Lee
Nectarines }

The Calphalon Kitchen

1# SORREL (from Maria)
Salad (small amount)
arugula
1# YV Kon gold
some other potatoes
* Buy small hot red peppers
string for the winter
← red

Bunch of bell peppers
roast & freeze for
yogurt
skim-milk
Tomatoes from Tim —
Brandywine
and few others
3 bun basil (don't get
it from Kenny. Pay for
Joan D Stokes
or Keith)

Cherry
Kirby
YG
red
okra

Onions
Eggplants
Basil / only
from
Anne
lie

beets
lola rosso / oak lettuce
potatoes
watercress
corn
6 med. zucchini /
garlic
lemongrass (for corn)
lemon

Varie
fr
2. S